Copyright © 2016 by Lani Sharp
All rights reserved. This book or any portion thereof
may not be reproduced or used in any manner whatsoever
without the express written permission of the publisher
except for the use of brief quotations in a book review.

Printed in Australia

First Printing, 2016

ISBN 978-0-9945051-6-3

White Light Publishing House
6 Lincoln Way
Melton West, VIC, Australia 3337

www.whitelightpublishingau.com

❧ DEDICATION ☙

Dedicated to my Dad, now departed from this Earthly plane, the most inspiring Sagittarian in my Universe. Over 25 years ago you took your last breath, but your lessons and wisdom live on in mine. Thank you for your love, faith, philosophies, illuminations, teachings, inspiration, directness, lessons, and for being such a wonderful part of my journey. I feel so lucky to have had such a special early teacher and father as you.

17 December 1945 - 30 August 1989

Flying up there with the Archer's arrows.

ABOUT THE AUTHOR

☾ ★ ☽

Lani Sharp is a Natural Born Rebel who just also happens to be an Aquarian, who shunned 'conventional' astrology courses to pursue her own path in the wondrous, inspiring and ever-evolving field of cosmic forces and stellar influences. After failing to find a course or tutor that suited her needs, Lani set out on her own starry Magic Carpet adventure across the skies, partly to discover her own 'truths' about this ancient system, but mostly to prove that one can achieve absolutely anything, including and above all, their dream careers (or lifestyle), if they put their hearts and souls into it. A self-taught astrologer who takes the esoteric and spiritual approach to this much-loved popular art, she has been studying and effectively practising astrology since she was eight years old. When she is not writing about, channelling, practising or teaching astrology, she can be found living her dream life alternating somewhere between her home in Australia's stunning Tropical North or her second home in Victoria's beautiful Dandenong Ranges, enjoying tea parties with her highly imaginative Cancerian daughter, Allira, and their gnome and fairy friends, crystal-wishing, day-dreaming, believing in gnomes, pixies, angels, fairies, magic and miracles, honing her magickal * witchcraft skills, Moon-gazing, Sun-worshipping, Venus-channelling, Jupiter-drawing, assisting others to discover, unravel and follow their true spiritual paths … or of course walking across rainbows!

Not a mistake. Magick is a Wiccan variation of the word 'magic'.

★

ACKNOWLEDGEMENTS, CREDITS & GRATITUDE BLESSINGS

I would love to thank the following people and entities for their amazing contributions, interest, support and faith in me as I wrote the manuscripts for each of the twelve astrological Sun signs. Firstly, the biggest thank you go to my Mum, Sandra, and my stepdad, Barry, for their unending support, love, advice, daily Skype conversations, acceptance of our geographical distance, and above all, their inner knowing that everything always comes together in the end. Your support of me and my dreams is appreciated beyond words. Secondly, gratitude to my wonderful partner, Travis, for his patience (no mean feat for a Gemini!), for supporting me every step of the way, and for his acceptance of my 'mad scientist' Aquarian mindset by never trying to break down the invisible 'laboratory' walls I built around myself while writing the books. I would also like to extend my enormous gratitude to the following: Allira, my little Cancerian 'crab' daughter, a soul in a billion, who also had to tolerate and operate within the bounds of her nutty professor mother's antics and focus throughout the writing of the books. Thank you to Nicola, my wonderful Facebook friend, for recommending White Light Publishing House, and of course to White Light Publishing House themselves, for pouring their faith and passion into my project from the very beginning - and an even bigger thank you to the wonderful people behind the company for publishing my work, Christie and Jess! Gratitude also goes out to my dear friends, both near and far, who have inspired in me so many ideas through simply being themselves - especially Amanda and Carlie. Amanda, you have always been my 'astrology buddy' and I have always enjoyed - and learned so much through - our discussions on all things astrology and star signs: the good, the bad and the ugly! Having someone like you off which to bounce thoughts and share ideas with, has always been immensely helpful and appreciated. I have saved my final thank you for The Universe, who always delivers to me exactly what I have asked for, without exception. The Universe is my ultimate *higher power*, my guiding light, my powerful driving force, my spiritual helper, my guardian angel, my eternal friend, my inner motivator, my sympathetic listener, my inspirational teacher, and the fulfiller of all my dreams, including this one, having my very first book(s) published, a long-held dream that stretches way back through the years to my days of being a mini dreamer, inquisitor and stargazer. The Universe has always believed in me, but perhaps more importantly, I have always believed in *IT*.

So to all of the above, I wish to say:

Thank you, thank you, thank you!

"We were born at a given moment, in a given place, and like vintage years of wine, we have the qualities of the year and of the season in which we are born"

Carl G. Jung

"There was a star danced,
and under that I was born"

William Shakespeare

INSPIRED BY ALL THE SIGNS

Aries imparted courage and boldness
And helped me dance away the pain
Taurus gave me hugs and comfort
And shelter from the rain
Gemini provided me with laughter
And taught me again how to have fun
Cancer nurtured and sustained me
By reflecting back my Sun
Leo reminded me there was joy
From within myself and above
Virgo awakened my healthy glow
By teaching me how to love
Libra gave me gentle hugs
And judged me not for a thing
Scorpio lent me some of his power
And took away the sting
Sagittarius showered me with gifts
Of words so wise and true
As Capricorn led the way up the mountain
My resolve and strength grew
Aquarius gave me the gift of friendship
And carried me as his brother
And Pisces swam with me to the depths
With a compassion like no other.

Special Note

Throughout the text of this book, and indeed the whole Lucky Astrology book series, I have capitalised the first letter of the word 'Universe'. This is because, quite simply, I feel it is a very special title for the higher power that I personally choose to be guided by, and have accordingly highlighted it as such.

You may also notice that I use the words 'he' or 'she', and 'his' or 'her', when referring to your own Sun sign and other zodiac signs, and never 'he or she' or 'his or her' together. The reason for this is for simplicity, for I don't wish the sentences to be too wordy and therefore the messages within them to be lost. As a general rule, I refer to all six 'masculine' zodiac signs as 'he', and all six 'feminine' signs as 'she', and this remains a consistent rule throughout this book and the whole series.

Your Sun sign, Sagittarius, is a masculine sign and will thus be referred to accordingly.

CONTENTS

	Page
ASTROLOGY	15
THE ZODIAC & YOUR PLACE IN THE SUN	24
SAGITTARIUS THE ARCHER	31
QUOTES BY SAGITTARIANS	37
THE SAGITTARIUS CONSTELLATION	42
THE SAGITTARIUS SYMBOL	45
THE RUNDOWN & LESSONS ★	
THE ESSENCE OF SAGITTARIUS	48
THE THREE DECANS OF SAGITTARIUS	57
YOUR ELEMENT ★ FIRE	61
YOUR MODE ★ MUTABLE	84
YOUR RULING PLANET ★ JUPITER	87
YOUR HOUSE IN THE HOROSCOPE ★	
THE NINTH HOUSE	102
YOUR OPPOSITE SIGN ★ GEMINI	106
MAGIC, DRAWING, ATTRACTION, SPELLS, RITUALS, WISHING & POWER	115
ASTROLOGY & MAGIC	120
PLANETS ★ DAYS OF THE WEEK & THEIR POWERS	126
YOUR NATAL MOON PHASE	130
SPELLS, MAGIC & WISHING WITH MOON PHASES	133
THE MOON ★ WHAT T REPRESENTS IN THE HUMAN PSYCHE & NATAL CHART	140
YOUR MOON SIGN	143
YOUR BODY & HEALTH	153
THE CELL SALTS ★ ASTROLOGICAL TONICS	158

	Page
FIRE SIGN SAGITTARIUS & THE CHOLERIC HUMOUR	161
MONEY ATTRIBUTES	164
COLOURS ★ YOUR LUCKY COLOURS	167
LUCKY CAREER TIPS	181
LUCKY PLACES	186
GEMS & CRYSTALS	188
SAGITTARIAN POWER CRYSTALS	200
YOUR LUCKY NUMBERS	209
YOUR LUCKY MAGIC HOURS OR TIME UNITS	218
YOUR LUCKY DAY ★ THURSDAY	223
YOUR LUCKY CHARM / TALISMANS	227
YOUR LUCKY ANIMALS & BIRDS	230
YOUR METALS	245
PLANTS, HERBS, SPICES, TREES, SHRUBS, FLOWERS, SCENTS & INCENSE	247
YOUR FOODS	253
YOUR LUCKY WOOD & CELTIC TREE ★ OAK & ELDER	255
THE POWER OF LOVE	262
LUCKY IN LOVE? SAGITTARIUS COMPATIBILITY	275
YOUR TAROT CARDS	292
LUCKY 13 TIPS	313
HAVE YOU PACKED YOUR MAGICAL BAG FOR THE JOURNEY?	316
A FINAL WORD ★ TAPPING INTO THE MAGIC OF SAGITTARIUS	317

★ ASTROLOGY ★

Astrology: "Divination through the correlation of earthly events with celestial patterns"
'Real Magic', I. Bonewits, 1971

A BRIEF HISTORY

Astrology can be defined as the calculation and meaningful interpretation of the positions and motions of the heavenly bodies, and their correlation with human experiences. Its central concept is based upon this interconnectedness or correspondence between the stars and ourselves.

The word astrology is derived from the Greek word astron, meaning 'star' and logos which means 'word'. Astrology, therefore, literally means language of the stars. It is based on the ancient law known as 'As Above, So Below', otherwise known as the Law of the Macrocosm and Microcosm. The Macrocosm is the Universe, symbolised by the sky, the starry dome that we can see from the Earth; the Microcosm is us - humans, and all other life on Earth. 'As Above, So Below' is a well-known and deeply impressing maxim of Hermetic origin, inscribed upon the famed Emerald Tablet among cryptic wording by enigmatic figure, Hermes Trismegistus, around 5,000 years ago. These four powerful words are adopted by astrologers and believers in magic to explain, in very succinct wording, the meaning behind the art and science of celestial influences upon our Earthly affairs.

Astrology and many other magical and occult studies, propose that we are not separate from the Universe, we are part of it. The Sun, Moon and planets all follow exact patterns of movement and their motions can be measured precisely by astronomers. The basic idea of astrology is that all individual parts of the Universe, from plants to animals, cooperate with each other and work together in harmony.

Anyone can apply astrological knowledge in their daily lives, but it hasn't always been like that. At one time, astrology was reserved only for Kings and nations, and only the court astrologer/astronomer could cast and interpret horoscopes. Ancient astrology and astronomy used to be one and the same. To be an astrologer, you first had to be able to interpret the stars in some systematic way, and then track the movement of the Moon and the planets against the background of the constellations.

Astrology, the knowledge and language of the cosmos, goes back to the ancient kingdom of Babylonia and was adapted by the Mesopotamians, Greeks, Egyptians and Romans to incorporate their own deities (as indicated in mythology). It is upon a combination of Greek and Egyptian interpretations of astrology that our present knowledge is based.

In the ancient Mesopotamian world, as far back as 800 BC, people lived precariously beneath the open skies. The skies and the stars which filled them, were the real founders of astrology. Today we are aware that the Sun and Moon exert a profound influence upon our Earthly affairs, but for our primitive ancestors, the heavens, the stars and the planets must have been a matter of great and mysterious significance. Early humankind, its senses influenced by natural processes of ebbs, flows, growth, decay and cycles, tended naturally towards a physical explanation of the Universe. At first, the movements of the planets - and all celestial occurrences - were observed as omens affecting the Ruler and his nation; it was only in Egypt in the fifth century AD that the casting of horoscopes for individual people and the calculation of the planetary positions at the time of birth became widespread.

The first astrologers, the Chaldeans, mapped the stars and later passed this knowledge and wisdom on to the ancient Greeks, who, during the third century BC, developed astrology into a science with the use of mathematical aids and instruments to measure planetary movements. The Greeks were the first to cast individual horoscopes. And it was the Greeks who associated the four elements with the signs of the zodiac. The word "zodiac" can be translated from Greek to mean the "circle or path of the animals." The Greeks not only had names for the twelve Solar phases but had symbols for each, and many correspond with the ones we use today.

The Greeks passed on much of their knowledge to the Romans. During the second century BC, Roman astrologers were primarily forecasters who were consulted frequently by rulers of the church and state. By the early third century AD, astrology co-existed with early Christianity. This harmonious co-existence was possible because it was considered that celestial bodies could foretell events, but did not determine the future - indeed, the stars seen by the shepherds at the time of Christ's birth were only predictors of his arrival. After the fourth century AD, Christianity strengthened and the popularity of astrology declined as Christian reluctance to support 'pagan' or 'superstitious' beliefs became more prominent. The Middle Ages saw a revival in astrology, with courses being taught in universities and other educational establishments, and connections were made between the zodiac, alchemy, herbs and medicine. Astrology was once again able to exist alongside the Church, although many remained suspicious of astrologers.

Around the beginning of the fifteenth century, academics of the Renaissance movement examined the past for knowledge, and ancient philosophies, including astrology, flourished; this coincided with arts and science movements developing. The famous prophet and astrologer Nostradamus lived during this period. Leonardo da Vinci depicted aspects of astrology combined with geometry in his art. Writers and poets of the time, including Shakespeare, alluded to zodiacal influences in their work.

During this period, astrology had numerous practical applications. Agricultural calendars were introduced, indicating favourable planting times according to the phases of the Moon; health and illness were linked with movements of celestial bodies; and emotional states and mental health afflictions correlated with the planetary positions.

Eventually, new ways of thinking led to a split between astronomy and astrology, and by the seventeenth century, the realm of science had developed to such a degree that astrology was no longer taken seriously.

The study of the sky above us has been charted for more than 5,000 years. This fact is known because ancient 'horoscopes' imprinted on clay tablets have been unearthed, dating back almost 5,400 years ago. However, no one knows for certain just how, when and where astrology first began, although it is known that it flourished in ancient Chaldea, Mesopotamia, Babylon and Egypt.

Astrology is a science which has spanned many centuries and still remains extraordinarily popular, and its truths have the potential to speak to and *through* all of us. Long before today's interest in it, men of great vision such as Ptolemy, Hippocrates, Plato, Galileo, Jefferson, Franklin, Newton, Columbus and Jung respected its inherent truths, mythology and eternal knowledge. Furthermore, astrology predates many other 'sciences' - for out of it grew religion, medicine and astronomy, not the other way around.

The discipline of astrology is ultimately a study of the interlocking and interrelated forces of the twelve zodiacal forces, or constellations, that grace the heavens, as they pour their energies into the Earthly kingdoms below. As these various energies circulate throughout the etheric realm of our Solar system, these zodiacal entities and archetypes imprint their vibrational frequencies and harmonic resonances upon our bodies, minds, souls and spirits.

ASTROLOGY & THE INDIVIDUAL

Since the earliest period of the history of humankind, people studied the starry vaults of the heavens and conceived that their presence, movements and positions endowed planet Earth's inhabitants with Divine influence. There is much evidence that positions and movements of the planets as seen from Earth at the time of a birth are linked to personality characteristics of individuals. Human energy and emotional cycles are governed by the forces and networks of magnetic impulses from all the planets. Of all the heavenly bodies, the Moon's effects and power are the most marked and visible due to its close proximity to Earth. But the Sun, Venus, Mars, Mercury, Jupiter, Saturn, Uranus, Neptune and Pluto exercise their influences just as surely. In fact, scientists are aware that plants and animals are affected by natural cycles which are governed by forces such as fluctuations in barometric pressure, the gravitational field and electricity in the air. These Earthly dynamics are originally triggered by magnetic vibrations from the atmosphere, or outer space, from where the planets send forth their unseen waves. No living organism or mineral on Earth escapes these immense, if unseen, influences.

The geomagnetic field seems to affect life on Earth in certain observed ways, and these influences appear to correlate with planetary positions. It has been suggested that the fluctuations of the Earth's magnetic field are picked up by the nervous system of the in utero infant, which acts like an antenna, and these synchronise the internal biological clocks of the foetus which control the moment of birth. The foetal magnetic antenna therefore, is sensitive enough to sense these planetary vibrations and fields, and through a combination of inherited genetics and the positions of the planets at birth, they are imprinted with certain basic inherited and 'absorbed' personality characteristics.

Carl Jung, the Swiss psychiatrist and psychological theorist, suggested that the inherent disposition of the individual is present at birth, and is reflected in the patterns of his or her natal chart. Further, he theorised that there is a 'priori factor' in all human activities, namely the inborn, preconscious and unconscious individual structure of the psyche. The preconscious psyche, for example that of a newborn baby, is not simply an empty vessel into which practically anything can be poured, but rather it is this preconscious psyche that gives us the free will to become what we are instead of what others or our environment makes us. The child is not merely a receptacle for the psychic life of those around him or her, albeit sensitive and susceptible to the surrounding unconscious forces in childhood; for he/she also brings something of his own to his experience of them.

Further, Dr Harold S. Burr, who was a Professor of Anatomy at the Yale University School of Medicine, and author of *The Nature of Man and the Meaning of Existence* (1962), asserted that there is order in the Universe, unity in the organism and man is endowed with a soul. He stated that a complex magnetic field not only establishes the pattern of the human brain at birth, but continues to regulate and control it through life, and that the human central nervous system is a superb receptor of electro-magnetic energies, indeed the finest in nature. He contended that the electro-dynamic fields of all living things, which may be measured and mapped with standard voltmeters, mould and control each organism's development, health and mood, and named these fields 'fields of life'.

It can therefore be suggested that astrological and planetary influences endow us with the majority of our characteristics at birth, characteristics bestowed upon us according to our Sun sign and other planetary forces. Other parts of the chart are also highly significant and need to be integrated for a 'whole' picture to form, however the Sun sign is an excellent starting point.

The ancients taught that astrology was one of the keys to the many enigmas that plague humans in their unceasing quest to determine what the meaning of life is, and what their role and place in the Universe is - and this quest still persists today. Astrology, which dates back over 5,000 years, is indeed one such key to unlocking the many secrets of the Universe - and ultimately, the individual self.

"KNOW THYSELF"

Man, know thyself. All wisdom centres on this.
Carl Jung

Before the temple of the Oracle at Delphi, the ancient Greeks imparted a special piece of advice that was carved onto one of the portals: "Know Thyself." These two powerful words are easy enough to understand, but much more difficult to apply. Throughout life's inner and outer journey, astrology can provide us with an inner navigational system by which we can be guided towards our highest potential, and closer towards the eternal quest of 'knowing thyself'. It provides the hope that this higher spiritual plane exists and that if we can 'read' and therefore be guided by the unique inner blueprint that our individual birth chart has stamped upon us at the moment we take our very first breath, indeed we can reach this higher spiritual plane and realise our innate potential.

Always remember that astrology is not fatalistic. The stars may incline, but they do not compel. Astrology simply provides us with an inner guide, a blueprint, for our journey through life and the finding of our true selves - and what we do with the resulting knowledge is entirely up to us.

Good luck on your journey!

THE ZODIAC & YOUR PLACE IN THE SUN

The zodiac is a circle of 360 degrees, consisting of equal segments of 30 degrees each. These represent the twelve houses of the twelve astrological signs. This zodiac is how the early astrologers imagined the Solar system to be, a perfect circle with the Earth at its centre, around which the Sun, Moon and the planets revolved. Each sign of the zodiac corresponds to one of the twelve segments, following a chronological order and established according to the rhythm of the seasons and cycles of the Sun and the Moon. But the zodiac itself, or the band of constellations which comprise it, has shifted over the millennia, creating division between astronomical and astrological schools of thought. It has been said that due to this shift over time, one who once considered themselves as an Aquarian, is actually a Capricorn, the sign before it, and a Leo is actually a Cancerian, its preceding sign. This is the result of misunderstandings and differences in perspectives, and explanations around it are beyond the scope of this book, but can be researched further should you wish to delve a little deeper. From the astronomical point of view, it is true that the zodiac to which we refer today is not situated where it 'should' be, but indeed, nothing is fixed under the celestial vault. And so the starting point of the ancient zodiac does not correspond exactly to the one we can observe today. But for the purposes of increasing your power and luck, let's keep things simple and enjoy the ride; after all, astrology - while based upon many scientific theories, mysteries, scepticism, superstitions, facts, measurable patterns, ambiguities, correlations, paradoxes, contradictions, links, stigmatisms and observations that seek to support, refute, prove and disprove this ancient art time and again - is ultimately meant to be *fun* too!

THE SUN

Earth's Luminary ★ *Our Brightest Shining Star*

Our Centre, Core Self, Identity & Inner Guiding Light

"Perfect is what I have said of the work of the Sun."
Hermes Trismegistus, *The Emerald Tablet*

The Sun is our essence, centre, source, ego strength, power, life force, will, vitality, creative expression, purpose, life's direction, our sense of identity, and who we really *are*. Our brightest star is the core of our individuality, our inner guiding light. The Sun is externalising, and represents totality, infinity, eternity, the striving toward and ultimate reaching of one's personal destiny, and *completion* in all areas. It is the creative energising giver of life and the 'father' of the zodiac. It endows us with our inherent creative potential and personal identity - our urge to *create* and to *be*. The Sun is our core self, conscious purpose, our sense of creating something out of our own being. It is the integrated personality and represents the *present*, our greatest Gift. The Sun rules the heart and is thus symbolically the centre of self. Indeed, the Sun *is* the heart and the most commanding presence in our birth chart; the luminary Ruler who governs our essential self and wants to be noticed and appreciated, and above all, to *shine*.

★ KEY WORDS ★

Identity, core self, spirit, life force, power, essence, creativity, higher self, the Father, ego, vitality, pride, individuality, leadership, majesty, inner authority, will, expression, willpower, purpose, the journey, the path and the destiny.

THE SUN ★ THE ULTIMATE SOURCE OF LIFE ON EARTH

Throughout the ages, and indeed since life forms began, the electromagnetic waves generated by the Sun have kept planet Earth habitable for humans, animals, plants and minerals. The Sun is, in fact, the only true source of energy on planet Earth. It provides the perfect amount of energy for plants to synthesise all of the products required for growth and reproduction, which is then stored by plants and ingested by humans and animals who, through many complex processes, utilise these various forms of encapsulated Solar energy - and so the cycle continues. Wood, fuel and minerals (crystals included), too, are merely various forms of this encased Sun energy. In fact all matter is essentially 'frozen' light. Human body cells are bundles of Sun energy; we couldn't conceive or process a single thought without the molecules of Solar-energised oxygen and glucose.

In essence, the Sun supports the growth of all species, including human beings and microscopic life forms, and without it life on Earth would simply not be possible. The mathematical and metaphysical complexity that stands behind a system of organisation and order so infinitely diverse and intricate as planetary life cannot be truly fathomed, but unerringly and miraculously, the Sun instinctively knows what each species, from a tree to a human, intrinsically needs in order to fulfil its evolutionary purpose and cycles.

Ultimately, the electromagnetic waves generated by the Sun come in a variety of lengths, which determine their specific course of action and responsibility. There are gamma rays, x-rays, cosmic rays, various kinds of ultraviolet rays, infrared, short-wave infrared, radio waves, electric waves, and of course the visible light spectrum, consisting of the seven colour rays.

Most of these energy waves are absorbed and used for various processes in the layers of atmosphere that encircle the Earth, and only a small portion of them - the electromagnetic spectrum - reach the surface of our planet. Although the human eye is only able to perceive about one percent of this spectrum, the waves exert a very strong influence upon us. The waves and rays which do affect us so profoundly, allow all life forms to undergo constant cycles of change necessary for growth and renewal. Physically, we can observe this, but on a deeper, more spiritual plane, we can even *feel* it and allow its radiance to permeate our very souls. Such is the might, force and power of that astonishing ball of fire in our sky: the brilliant, ever-shining Sun.

THE SUN ★ WHAT IT REPRESENTS IN THE HUMAN PSYCHE & NATAL CHART

☼

"The Sun is the most powerful of all the stellar bodies. It colours the personality so strongly that an amazingly accurate picture can be given of the individual who was born when it was exercising its power through the known and predicable influences of a certain astrological sign; these electromagnetic vibrations will continue to stamp that person with the characteristics of their Sun sign as they go through life."
Linda Goodman's Sun Signs, **Linda Goodman, Pan Books, 1968**

The Sun is our essence, our core self, conscious purpose and sense of identity, our creative potential, our spirit, the integrated personality that shines outward from within us. It is concerned with the present. It is our centre, source, power, life force, will, vitality, purpose, life's direction, what and who we *really* are.

The Sun represents our basic urge for self-expression. It is the 'Solar energy cell' in a person's character, the Lord and giver of life, and symbolises the way in which an individual will shine out to the world. Our Sun is our personal identity and aspects to it from other components in the chart show the ease or otherwise of assuredness and confidence with which one will project and express one's individuality. The Sun sign will also show how an individual bounces back from setbacks and disappointments, their resilience and their general outward expression of energy.

The Sun is the archetype of the Father and represents the primary masculine principle in the natal chart. It indicates how we express and experience our masculine side, or animus, our conscious self, how we express ourselves creatively, our personal potential, individuality, self-expression and personal power. It has to do with courage, power, generosity, creativity, vitality, self-confidence, nobility, self-worth, dignity and strength of will. It symbolises authority and purpose, the *ruler*, and its potential is the peak of constructive maturity. It signifies self-sufficiency and abundance, containing enough energy to radiate warmth and give life to everything around it.

The sign in which one's Sun is posited, and its placement in the birth chart, strongly indicates the level and type of vitality available to the personality (the sign), and in which area of life this may be most strongly directed (the house).

The Sun in a natal chart is a powerful symbol because everything is filtered, at a conscious level, through it. It tells us what we need to do to feel fully alive, the type of engine 'driving' us, what we need to do to be authentic and to be fully functioning. Listening to the special message of one's Sun sign can provide one with greater direction, and a more dynamic energy and life purpose.

The symbol for the Sun ☉ depicts a circle with a dot or 'seed' at its centre, from which the core self, power, creativity and the first sparks of life can spring. The circle around this 'seed' represents spirit, symbolising wholeness, eternity and the never-ending flow of energy.

While the Moon, the night sky's luminary, represents the *soul*, the Sun, the day sky's luminary, represents our *spirit*.

There is a reason your Sun sign is otherwise known as your Star Sign - it's because, quite simply, the Sun *is* a star; in fact, it's the largest, brightest, shiniest one in Earth's known visible Universe. This book is about your Sun sign and how you can become much larger, glow with far more brilliance, and shine brighter than you ever dreamed possible. I wish you all the magic in the galaxy for your dreams to come true and your deepest wishes to become reality, through tapping into the amazing power and inherent potential of your Sun sign. So get set for a galactical ride through the lucky stars of your constellation - and may a shooting star cross the path in front of you as you go!

SAGITTARIUS THE ARCHER

★ Mutable Fire, Masculine, Positive, Intuitive ★

"The arrow speeds on its quest to the far horizon"

Body & Health
Hips, Thighs, Liver, Sciatic Nerve, Blood,
Sacral Region, Gluteus Muscles

How Sagittarius Emanates its
Life Force / Energy
Idealistically, meaningfully, truthfully, with charm

Is Concerned With
★ Philosophy ★ Idealism ★ Religion ★ Spiritual Growth ★ Vision ★ Optimism ★ The Future ★ Positive Outlook ★ Travel ★ Freedom of Movement ★ The Great Outdoors ★ Generosity ★ Charm ★ Justice ★ Morality ★ Ethics ★ Aspirations ★ Higher learning ★ Open-mindedness ★ Romance ★ Flirting ★ Intellect ★ Wit ★ Pleasure ★ Truth ★ Expansion ★ Honesty ★ Sharing Ideas ★ Sociability ★

Spiritual Sagittarius

Your Archetypal Universal Qualities
The Philosopher, Explorer, Wise Teacher

What You Refuse
To be dishonest or immoral, or to stop believing

What You Are an Authority On
Faith, Optimism, Religion and Philosophy

The Main Senses Through Which You Experience Your Reality
Hope, Growth, Abundance, Clarity, Expansion, Righteousness, Vision, The Higher Mind

How You Love
Adventurously, Playfully, Charmingly

Positive Characteristics
★ Sociable ★ Charming ★ Optimistic ★ Warm ★
★ Frank, Open & Direct ★ Happy-go-lucky ★
★ Friendly ★ Approachable ★ Holds No Grudges ★
★ Sees the Best in Others ★ Enthusiastic ★
★ Honest ★ Fair-minded ★ Inspiring ★ Interesting ★
★ Spirited ★ Fun ★ Great Sense of Humour ★
★ Stimulating ★ Developed Sense of Wonder ★

Negative Characteristics
★ Argumentative ★ Opinionated ★ Fanatical ★
★ Non-committal ★ Irresponsible ★ Tactless ★
★ Impatient ★ Unreliable ★ A Gambler ★ Insensitive ★
★ Hot-headed ★ Fails to Plan ★ Careless ★ Unaware ★
★ Blunt ★ Insulting ★ Preaching ★ Undisciplined ★
★ Fears Responsibility that Curtails Freedom ★
★ Indulgent ★ Extravagant ★ Blundering ★
★ Denies Negative Emotions ★ Inept ★ Clumsy ★

To Bring Out Your Best

Travel, especially to foreign places; study a subject of interest in depth; undertake adventure sports and activities; drink expensive wine; develop your culture and sophistication; share philosophical ideas with like-minded others; throw dinner parties for stimulating intellectual exchanges.

Spiritual Goals

To learn to stop fearing the loss of freedom; to use your talents to guide and be an example to others; to be more tactful and sensitive; to exercise more responsibility and care in everything you do; to be more committed and less flighty.

SAGITTARIUS

22 November - 21 December

Mutable Fire

Ruled by Jupiter

"I AIM"

Gemstones ◊ Topaz, Zircon, Turquoise

★ Outgoing, optimistic, risk-taker, jovial, independent, traveller, freedom-loving, broad-minded, blunt, impulsive, outdoorsy, higher learner, fun, sociable, bold, intolerant of ignorance, fun, open-minded, honourable, reckless, sincere, direct, reasonable, impatient, outspoken, flirtatious, honest, flighty, philosophical, non-committal, cheerful, enthusiastic, clumsy, exaggerated, untidy, tactless, adventurous ★

"Some of the worst mistakes of my life have been haircuts"
Jim Morrison

SAGITTARIUS

♐

**★ Bold ★ Freedom-seeking ★ Fun ★
Confident ★ Charming ★ Optimistic ★
★ Direct ★ Sociable ★**

Sagittarius is the sign of the Archer, an upwards shooting Centaur who aims its arrow towards higher meaning and ideals. Optimistic, expansive, independent, fun, sociable, cheerful, blunt, confident, freedom-loving, philosophical and broadminded are Sagittarius' most notable traits. Being a fabulous Fire sign, this sign burns brightly but will take its flame to new horizons if its freedom, higher truth-seeking or need for new stimulation is curtailed in any way. Bold and direct, Sagittarius loves to be the jovial life of the party, entertaining with his wit and impressing with his effortless charm. The Archer can sometimes offend more sensitive souls with his brash and outspoken expression, but his cheerful and clever disposition will usually mean he is easily forgiven by the next joke. Adventure and travel are big things for the outgoing Archer's spirit, and he needs plenty of new and novel places and people to explore to keep his fire and passion burning. Sagittarius is flirtatious and charming, but his independence, flightiness and love of freedom can make him an unreliable long-term partner. A dynamic lover, fun-loving friend and a reckless and fearless risk-taker, Sagittarius is the ninth sign and the far-travelling philosopher of the zodiac, skipping through life without a care and whistling a happy tune which can brighten up the dullest of days and the heaviest of hearts!

KEY CONCEPTS

★ Vast and inspirational mind ★
★ Gregarious, humane and sociable ★
★ Broad-minded vision ★
★ Inability to integrate mind with matter ★
★ Exaggerating ★
★ Generous and magnanimous ★
★ Expansive but gluttonous, never satisfied ★
★ Boisterous and coarse ★
★ Propagandist, zealot and dictator ★
★ Bold, direct and straightforward ★
★ Aimless and wandering ★
★ Citizen of the world ★
★ The wise teacher and judge ★

SOME CORRESPONDENCES THAT ARE ASSOCIATED WITH SAGITTARIUS

Explorers, archery, horses, lawyers, spirituality, philosophy, cheerfulness, sportspeople, higher education, foreign ambassadors, universities, custodians, the great outdoors, independence, cathedrals, religion, churches, the legal profession, preachers, foreign people and places, exporting, humour, hips and thighs, judges, religious practitioners, long journeys, tin, importing, adventure, the liver, publishing, optimism, hunting, airline hostesses and stewards, faith, customs departments and officers, race horses, wide open spaces, and freedom. Take your pick and enjoy the ride!

QUOTES BY SAGITTARIANS

"It is the soul's duty to be loyal to its own desires. It must abandon itself to its master passion" - Rebecca West (21 December 1892)

"It's never too late to be who you might have been" - George Eliot (22 November 1819)

"Always tell the truth. It's the easiest thing to remember" - David Mamet (30 November 1947)

"I'm working my way towards divinity" - Bette Midler (1 December 1945)

"After there is great trouble among mankind, a greater one is prepared. The great mover of the Universe will renew time, rain, blood, thirst, famine, steel weapons and disease. In the heavens, a fire seen" - Nostradamus (14 December 1503)

"I always liked those moments of epiphany, when you have the next destination" - Brad Pitt (18 December 1963)

"The magic of first love is our ignorance that it can ever end" - Benjamin Disraeli (21 December 1804)

"In attempts to improve your character, know what is in your power and what is beyond it" - Francis Thompson (16 December 1859)

"No one can possibly achieve real success by being a conformist" - J. Paul Getty (15 December 1892)

"My happiest moment is the day they call wrap and I'm free. I'm not looking back" - Brad Pitt

"Mind is the master. Power that moulds and makes man is mind and evermore he takes, the tool of though and shaping what he wills, brings forth a thousand joys, a thousand ills. He thinks in secret and it comes to pass. Environment is but his looking glass" - James Allen (28 November 1864)

"Never trust a man who when left alone with a tea cosy, doesn't try it on" - Billy Connolly (24 November 1942)

"Sometimes you've got to let everything go - purge yourself ... because you'll find that when you're free, your true creativity, your true self comes out" - Tina Turner (26 November 1939)

"Knowledge speaks, but wisdom listens" - Jimi Hendrix (27 November 1942)

"Expose yourself to your deepest fear; after that, fear has no power. You are free" - Jim Morrison (8 December 1943)

"Most people are anxious to improve their circumstances, but are unwilling to improve themselves. They, therefore, remain bound to their circumstances" - James Allen

"You take your problems to a god, but what you really need is for the god to take you to the inside of you" - Tina Turner

"The thankful receiver bears a plentiful harvest" - William Blake (28 November 1757)

"The greatest good you can do for another is not just share your riches, but reveal to them their own" - Benjamin Disraeli

"You are never too old to set another goal or to dream a new dream" - C.S. Lewis (29 November 1898)

"Did your mother never tell you not to drink on an empty head?" - Billy Connolly

"Music is my religion" - Jimi Hendrix

"Knowledge will give you power, but character respect" - Bruce Lee (27 November 1940)

"I see myself as an intelligent, sensitive human, with the soul of a clown which forces me to blow it at the most important moment" - Jim Morrison

"You have enemies? Good. That means you've stood up for something, some time in your life" - Winston Churchill (30 November 1874)

"Great things are done when men and mountains meet" - William Blake

"Eighty per cent of success is showing up" - Woody Allen (1 December 1935)

"When I sing, it's the most solitary state: just me, and the microphone, and the holy spirit. It's not about notes or scales, it's all about emotion" - Sinead O'Connor (8 December 1966)

"The key to immortality is first living a life worth remembering" - Bruce Lee

"There are things known and things unknown, and in between are the doors" - Jim Morrison

"Basically, I'm for whatever gets you through the night" - Frank Sinatra (12 December 1915)

"Success consists of going from failure to failure without loss of enthusiasm" - Winston Churchill

"Real poetry doesn't say anything; it just ticks off the possibilities. Opens all doors. You can walk through any one that suits you" - Jim Morrison

"You can live to be a hundred if you give up all the things that make you want to live to be a hundred" - Woody Allen

"I dream for a living" - Steven Spielberg (18 December 1946)

"We make a living by what we get, but we make a life by what we give" - Winston Churchill

"(Our lives will end), as they do in part, as we each refuse the opportunity to change - we stagnate and perform ever greater prodigies of repression and hypocrisy, to explain to ourselves why we don't immerse ourselves in the mysteries of life. We all die in the end, but there's no reason to die in the middle" - David Mamet

"The future enters into us in order to transform us, long before it happens" - Rainer Maria Rilke (4 December 1875)

"A pessimist sees the difficulty in every opportunity; an optimist sees the opportunity in every difficulty" - Winston Churchill

Twenty years from now you will be more disappointed by the things that you didn't do than by the ones that you did do. So throw off the bowlines. Sail away from the safe harbour. Catch the trade winds in your sails. Explore. Dream. Discover" - Mark Twain (30 November 1835)

"This is the strangest life I've ever known" - Jim Morrison

"All our dreams can come true, if we have the courage to pursue them" - Walt Disney (5 December 1901)

"Never, never, never give up" - Winston Churchill

THE SAGITTARIUS CONSTELLATION

The signs of the zodiac are the twelve symbolic features that ancient people imagined while observing the heavens. They saw shapes, patterns, faces, and natural and supernatural beings in the stars, from which they established, over centuries, a kind of celestial hierarchy and system based upon their observations. Groupings of stars became constellations, and twelve of these constellations make up the zodiac, a Greek word meaning 'circle of animals', that we know today.

Star constellations are not really self-contained groups but are particularly bright stars that give the appearance of being close together and form distinctive patterns. These are the patterns that over the ages have been identified as animals, deities or mythological figures and heroes. The stars are the living past. We receive their light long after it has left the star itself and so they are a good focus for escaping from the parameters of time. Their stellar influence is analogous with the aura, the bio/psychic energy field surrounding humans, animals, plants, crystals and even places. These individual energy systems interact with the energy waves emanated by other people, and even the cosmic rays emitted by planetary bodies, for psychic energies are not limited by time or distance.

The Sagittarius constellation is composed of eight bright but otherwise unremarkable stars, divided into two groups: the Milk Dipper, representing the

Centaur's body and the bow, and an additional star, Al-Nasl, which is the head of the arrow. The Centaur-Archer's arrow is aimed at Antares, the red heart of the Scorpion, his neighbour.

The cluster of stars we know as Sagittarius, is best seen in the Southern Hemisphere, because here the Milky Way is at its most impressive. Rising in the east after Scorpius, Sagittarius the Archer, a Centaur with his bow drawn, has his arrow pointing towards Scorpio's constellation. When we look at Sagittarius, we are looking towards the centre of our galaxy, so the sky here is thick with nebulae, stars and star clusters. Sagittarius lies in the centre of the Milky Way, and although the actual constellation is not outstanding from an astronomical point of view, its region in space is. Within the Archer's range is the huge Sagittarius stellar cloud, which is composed of millions of Suns and is easily seen with the naked eye for it is the Milky Way's brightest 'cloud'. Enormous nebulas and dark masses of cosmic dust that are so dense they obscure the space beyond them, can also be found here. Sagittarius also contains a globular star cluster which contains at least 50,000 stars (but to the naked eye appears as one large bright star) that are *each* probably greater in size than our own Sun.

WISHING UPON YOUR STAR

The practice of wishing upon a star is familiar to most of us, and is a mystical superstition that is ingrained in many of us from childhood. As a night-time ritual, you can wish upon your own sign's constellation or that of the sign whose energies you wish to call forth; indeed, you can wish upon any constellation you feel an affinity with. If you can't see a particular constellation in your night sky, you can always meditate on it in your mind, or you can use the traditional technique of wishing upon the first star you see, while reciting the popular rhyme: *Star light, star bright, first star I see tonight, I wish I may, I wish I might, have the wish I make this night!* Any one of the three rituals will hold power for your own special wish. Good luck!

THE SAGITTARIAN SYMBOL ♐

Astrology uses symbols or 'glyphs' to represent the planets and signs. The glyph is made up of shapes representing the energy and physical matter of which the Universe is composed, and how these shapes are used in each symbol provide hints as to the properties of the sign or planet it represents.

The ancient view was that there were five elements: Fire, Water, Air, Earth and Ether (or Spirit). Ether is invisible energy, while the four tangible elements are known as 'matter'. Ether, as pure energy, cannot be influenced by any of the physical/matter elements, although it surrounds them and indeed fuels them. The Greek philosopher and scientist Aristotle regarded this idea as a circle (Ether/Spirit) with a cross (matter) in the centre. This glyph is used in astrology as a symbol for Earth, and the cycle of life. All the symbols used in astrology represent the relationship between energy and the 'matter' elements.

The glyph of Sagittarius is the Arrow propelled from the bow of the Centaur, a mythical being, half man, half horse. The Horse, a symbol of the intuitive mind, is directed by the understanding of one's spirit, giving the power to develop true aim. The Arrow symbolises aspiration, which rightly directed, can lead one to his ultimate goal. The lower part of the shaft connotes the animal nature of this symbol, likened to the Centaur; the intersecting line dividing the shaft indicates duality or indecisiveness as to how or where to aim one's greatest physical and mental powers.

THE CENTAUR

The Centaur represents Sagittarius. A creature of dualities, it symbolises passion and intellect, instinct and animal nature. Unlike most hybrid beings, the Centaurs were based on the horse and the human. Part-human, part-animal beings in Greek mythology tend to be evil and aggressive, but because horses were regarded as being very noble creatures, Centaurs were more enlightened than most. Depicted with the torso and head of a man and the legs and lower body of a horse, they followed the wine god Dionysus and enjoyed drinking to excess, which stirred their passions. Centaurs were renowned for lechery and were often found crashing parties trying to steal the maidenhood of young females. Chiron, an important astrological 'planetoid', also known as 'the Wounded Healer', was different from all the other Centaurs in that he possessed great wisdom and dedicated himself to study that eventually led to him becoming one of the wisest of all the beings in Ancient Greece, particularly in the area of the healing arts. His sacrifices and wise counsel saw to it that Chiron was immortalised in the sky as the constellation of Sagittarius.

THE AGE OF SAGITTARIUS ★ 18,000 - 16,000 BC

The Age of Sagittarius saw the enlightenment and expansion of human cultures across the world. This age lies deep in human prehistory and we know little about the activities of the people during that period. We do know that humans had been using fire for some time, but it was during the Age of Sagittarius that fire was truly put to domestic use. Burning animal fats as fuel for lamps marked the beginning of the widespread use of artificial light in homes. Jupiter, the ruler of Sagittarius, is associated with enlightenment and in the Sagittarian Age light was literally utilised to further human endeavours, or at least extend the hours during which people could interact and exchange. Images of horses, a Sagittarian animal, survive in cave paintings from this period, and there were also many large animals at this time, such as the mighty mammoth, which would eventually evolve into much smaller variants of their species. The transformation of these beasts during this period reflects the mutable nature of Sagittarius. Many parts of the world, in particular eastern Asia, saw a massive expansion in population. It was also an age of travel, a Sagittarian-ruled concept, as people began to move further and wider, and settle in warmer climes.

THE RUNDOWN & LESSONS
SOME QUIRKS, ODDITIES, UNIQUE CHARACTERISTICS AND IDIOSYNCRASIES OF SAGITTARIUS

"Ah, but the Sagittarius-influenced man or woman isn't just any horse: he's Silver and the Lone Ranger combined ... Sagittarian types always know what's best for everybody, and they're not shy about saying so. They are the sheriff; we are the posse. (We should) gallop after our dauntless leader, who is absolutely certain where he's going even if it happens to be exactly opposite to where he thinks he's going to get. The beautiful self-assurance of the misaimed Sagittarian is a phenomenon which has to be experienced to be believed."
Astrology for Skeptics, **Charlotte MacLeod, The Macmillan Company, 1972**

"To the Sagittarian, life is secretly a circus, and he's the clown, rolling and tumbling through purple hoops in a sky-blue suit ... He curves his bow towards the sky. When he aims straight, he shoots higher than man can see - past the stars - to the place where all dreams are really born."
Linda Goodman

There are two types of thinkers: what I like to call 'right-brainers' and 'left-brainers'. The left hemisphere of the human brain deals with things such as control of speech, verbal functions, logic, reason, mathematics, linear concepts, details, sequences, the intellect and analysis; the right hemisphere is concerned with spatial, music, holistic, artistic concepts, as well as simultaneity and intuition. You could go on to say that the left brain is masculine or yang in quality, and the right brain is feminine or yin in quality. Based upon these very simplistic outlines, it can be further stated that Fire sign Sagittarius dwells mainly in the left hemisphere, with a healthy dose of right thrown in for good measure.

The passionate, active nature of Fire highlights spontaneity and adventure rather than caution and practicality. Sagittarius is largely motivated by freedom of movement in mind and in body. Positive, hot, dry, Choleric and bright, a flexible (Mutable) inspired (Fire) approach characterises the sign of Sagittarius.

Sagittarius is the last of the Fiery signs, is positive in magnetism, and is ruled by the happy-go-lucky and jovial planet Jupiter. People born under this sign are generally idealistic, cheerful, generous and optimistic. You confidently and energetically explore the larger physical realm through travel, and the mental realm through study, reading or formal education to gain knowledge. You pursue the areas of religion, metaphysics and philosophy to uncover the meaning of life, and being of the Mutable quality, often change your focus as your interests change.

Sagittarius is the unfettered, freedom-loving gypsy of the zodiac, whose restless spirit is hard to contain. Ruled by the ebullient, benevolent god of thunder and lightning Jupiter, you possess an inflationary tendency like your ruler, which drives you to expand your horizons to the uttermost limits.

Having set your sights, you then proceed to explore your territory to the fullest. This journey or quest may take you all your life. Your territory may be physical or it may be of the mind. Either way, you ultimately seek meaning. Explorations you undertake are usually of the mind, for you are an eternal seeker of wisdom and knowledge. You love to disseminate and promulgate any wisdom acquired, and you love to teach, as a way of handing over the torch.

For such an optimistic, uncommitted and easy going person, you are surprisingly highly principled, ethical and idealistic, for you have a strong sense of justice and truth. Your insistence on speaking this truth can lead you into tactlessness, but there is never any deliberate intention to cause pain or unease. What is on your mind and in your heart, is almost immediately on your lips. You are as frank and earnest as a child, and it could even be said that with your stark honesty, if people want to hear the truth, they should seek out a Sagittarian. But few can resent you for very long, because you are so transparently free of any harmful intent. You usually speak and act first, and consider the consequences later. You may offend through carelessness, but never callousness, as you are generous, lovable, intelligent, affectionate and invariably good-humoured.

Inside anyone who has a strong Sagittarius influence in their natal chart, is someone who wants to be free. Possessive partners, jealous friends and stifling acquaintances may see them running for the nearest hills. The typical Sagittarius is a freedom and truth-seeker who will stop at nothing to keep these within easy reach. A Sagittarian who is held back,

LESSONS TO BE LEARNED FOR GREATER POWER, ENLIGHTENMENT & LUCK

Sagittarian problems and ultimate undoings arise through your seeking of freedom over commitment, the resulting untrustworthiness and unreliability, your carelessness and recklessness, failure to consider others' viewpoints if it jeopardises your independence of thought or movement, and your irresponsibility and tactlessness, however unintentional. You are far from dependable, making promises in the heat of the moment, then forgetting them in your constant pursuit of new adventures, wider horizons and greener fields. You can be insincere, boastful and downright blunt, offending the more sensitive of the signs, again without ill-intention but upsetting others nonetheless. If pushed to your limits, you can be sarcastic, cutting and spiteful. You need to learn how to effectively keep your word and follow through with promises, and curb your preposterousness by learning how to accommodate others more. Learning to commit and to compromise in a relationship is also something you may need to develop in order to experience more fulfilling relationships.

Your extroverted cheerfulness and attraction to abstract ideas and philosophies are the basis of your strengths *and* your weaknesses. At your highest level, you effortlessly walk and talk your truth - confidently, generously, humanely and philosophically. And living enthusiastically and loving life tend to bring you success and the fruition of your dreams and ambitions as a natural by-product. However, that same expansive idealism can lead to an excess of abstraction and carelessness. Wastefulness, extravagance, aimlessness, meaningless chatter, wandering attention, and endlessly doing things without apparent direction or purpose, can all result and make your character lazy and overly carefree. Used positively, your agile mind can boost the entire world and others' lives and you bring the gifts of true Spirit - inspiration, leadership, mentorship, self-respect, integrity and courage. It is only then that your happiness is infectious and uplifts others. You will also find your emotional security when you can focus on your common humanity with all people and find the correct limits for your ambitions and seemingly indiscriminate generosity. Making a conscious effort to find your authentic purpose and follow that path consistently, is key.

THE THREE DECANS OF SAGITTARIUS

Decans are thirty-six groups of stars that rise in a particular order on the horizon throughout each Earth rotation. These decans were developed in Egypt thousands of years ago. The rising of each decan marked the beginning of a new 'decanal hour' of the night for these ancient people, and eventually three decans were assigned to each zodiac sign. Each decan covers ten degrees of the zodiac wheel, and is ruled by different planetary rulers that rule over the other two signs of the same element (and a traditional ruler, when only seven of the planetary bodies were known). Decans continued to be used throughout the Ages, in astrology and in magic, but many modern astrologers, for whatever reasons, tend to disregard them. Following are brief descriptions for each decan of Sagittarius. Which one do you belong to? Can you relate to the description and the energies of your decan's ruling planet?

FIRST DECAN SAGITTARIUS ★ November 22 - December 1

Ruler ★ Mercury (traditional *) / Jupiter (modern)

Keyword ★ Wise

First Decan Sagittarius's Three Special Tarot Cards Temperance, Knight of Wands & Eight of Wands

Birthdays in this decan range from 22nd November to 1st December. This is the Sagittarius decan, ruled by Mercury * and Jupiter. Sagittarians born during this decan possess an honest, clever, idealistic and generous character. Your idealism can get the better of you sometimes, and you flee from complications and conflicts; you would prefer life and relationships to be breezy, simple and easy. With an agile, quick mind and a benevolent nature, you whiz through life taking on opportunities and soaking up learning and knowledge like a sponge. Freedom-seeking and independent, you are bold, restless and sociable, attracting people to you with your gregarious, straightforward and fun-loving manner. The combination of Mercurial and Jupiterian influences endows you with an enviable wisdom and philosophical bent that you use to advance your mission in life; people stand up and take notice when you have something to say. Although extremely enlightened, spontaneous, good-natured and ingenious, you are also inclined to be non-committal, flighty and a little cheeky at times, often putting your foot in your mouth and unsettling other more sensitive souls with your direct bluntness. You do, however, have a way with words and if you can use this talent to good ends, you will succeed at whatever it is you choose to do.

SECOND DECAN SAGITTARIUS ★
December 2 - 12

Ruler ★ Moon (traditional *) / Mars (modern)

Keyword ★ Adventurous

Second Decan Sagittarius's Three Special Tarot Cards Temperance, Knight of Wands & Nine of Wands

Birthdays in this decan range from 2nd December to 12th December. This is the Aries decan, ruled by the Moon * and Mars. These influences combine to make a curious combination, with Mars' usual warrior-like tendencies being softened somewhat by the Moon's presence. You will still show headstrong and impulsive mannerisms though, and have an instinctive urge to explore, expand spiritually and have fun. With a driven and insatiable urge to acquire knowledge, you are likely to be stimulated by an interest and curiosity in mysteries and the unseen, and an overall quest for knowledge. Endowed with a sympathetic and sincere kindness, you have a taste for adventure, travel, romance and friendships based on natural camaraderie. You are usually clear about what you want in life, but your usual decisiveness and assertiveness can sometimes be clouded by poor judgement, and your head and heart will often conflict when it comes to important decisions.

THIRD DECAN SAGITTARIUS ★ December 13 - 21

Ruler ★ Saturn (traditional *) / Sun (modern)

Keyword ★ Knowledge

Third Decan Sagittarius's Three Special Tarot Cards
Temperance, Queen of Pentacles & Ten of Wands

Birthdays in this decan range from 13th December to 21st December. This is the Leo decan, ruled by the Sun. This may add a more fixed energy to the natural restlessness of Sagittarius, and signifies achievement, charisma, publicity and showmanship. With the Leo influence, a love of the limelight, a tendency to take risks, intuition, loyalty and boldness are most likely part of your make-up. You have strong convictions and yearn to deepen your knowledge, a quest you remain ever devoted to. Demonstrative and affectionate, you win others over with a natural, albeit serious, charm. People born of this decan are truthful and bold, and you usually succeed in anything you aim your arrow towards, due to your astute negotiation skills. Warm, friendly, and with a love of publicity and the spotlight, you will never shy away from taking risks, for to you, life is one big, grand adventure which must be treated seriously and with great reverence.

* The decan's traditional ruler based on the Chaldean order of the planets

★ KEYWORDS ★

Adventurous, energetic, ardent, independent, passionate, enthusiastic, optimistic, impulsive, honest, exuberant, self-motivated, physical, individualistic, assertive, inspirational, courageous, has faith, spirited, warm, takes initiative, confident, extroverted, spontaneous, impatient, restless, simple and direct in approach, creative, idealistic, freedom-seeking, dramatic, forceful, Joi de Vivre! *

* All these words don't necessarily describe all three Fire signs. Leo, for example, is not necessarily restless or freedom-seeking.

Fire is fundamentally different to the other three elements, but it is the essential fourth. The other elements are eternal - only Fire has a birth and a death. Fire is ephemeral; even the blazing, glowing ball in the sky, our Sun, will burn out in time. Remember also that you need to nurture and replenish this primal force of expression, as fire is not self-sustaining and it needs fuel to maintain its heat, light, movement and momentum. Fire is, quite simply, the element of creation, the life force made manifest. The most active and consuming astrological energy, it is the element of spirit, roaming far and wide in search of inspiration and meaning. Fire is also the identity principle. It animates, transmutes and energises.

Fire is associated with the intuitive function and its motivating force is inspiration. Characterised by movement, force and energy, it offers new possibilities, regeneration and a buoyant, spontaneous expression. Fire's essential characteristic is the energetic exploration of life: to conquer, to lead and to travel - both mentally and physically. Fire signs are creative and perceptive, experiencing life through intuition and spirit. Fire is a conceptual and visionary element, ever searching for meaning. Its energy can light up the world, or scorch it out of existence. Stimulating and spontaneous, it has a warm, passionate, enthusiastic and active approach to life. Fire initiates and motivates, and it is optimistic and explorative. Fire is also connected with heroism, a sense of beginning, regrowth and the future. Aries represents personal development, Leo represents interpersonal development, and Sagittarius represents transpersonal development. They are masculine polarity, extroverted in action.

Fire is strength, power, protection, and the ability to change from one state to another. It is enlightenment and extremely potent but, like Air, it can represent truth and knowledge through purification. The alchemical sigil for Fire is an upright triangle, a male symbol meaning action and movement. Pointing upwards, it represents the path to higher truths, light and transformation through self-motivated activity. But like any magical elemental energy, Fire has two sides: creation and destruction. It can destroy things for the better, such as the symbolic 'burning away' of old thought patterns, bad habits, negativity, and things we no longer need in our lives.

The Fire element is spiritual, progressive, transcending, visionary, confident, 'birthing', associated with starting points, and a sense of the Divine, is reactive, has faith, philosophical, quests for purpose, is playful, joyful, connected to the 'inner child', ascending, optimistic, combative, has a strong expression of emotions, is straightforward, direct, spontaneous, risk-taking, passionate, forceful, dynamic, bold, humorous, idealistic, and intuitive in the perceiving sense, not the feeling sense.

As the element suggests, Fire signs are a great source of warmth, intensity and light, but they can also be volatile. Exuberant, passionate and motivated, Fire signs are the active people of the zodiac, preferring to lead and take initiative rather than wait for things to happen. Blessed with confident, fun-loving and dynamic personalities, they have a natural flair for boosting talent, morale and confidence, and are usually the driving force behind relationship and family decisions. Fire signs are the extroverts of the zodiac, being charismatic, enthusiastic and assertive, usually being the first to make an introduction, explore wider horizons or conquer new ground. While their natural positivity and optimism can be infectious, they may also be inadvertently selfish, overbearing, bossy and over-zealous in their approach. The passionate Fire signs also like stimulation and drama, and in the absence of excitement, may wander elsewhere to find it. Being impulsive, they may take risks and be compelled to act and speak without thinking, coming across as reckless, careless and tactless. Although honest and direct, they may have a tendency to be blunt. Charming but impatient and impetuous, Fire signs have an admirable lust for life, immense bravery, enormous generosity of spirit, and a fierce and protective loyalty towards their loved ones.

"To be alive is to be burning," asserted psychoanalyst Norman O. Brown. Too much burning, however, can lead to burnout. Too much unrestrained Fire can burn others. When Fire people are out of control, fire extinguishers (water) and stamping it out with a heavy material (Earth) can work wonders. Fire generated by a spark can spread as a forest fire spreads, creating excessive heat and smoke, which can sear and smother.

However, the inner heat that Fire provides is the sustaining life force that contributes to self-confidence, radiance, eagerness, faith, forward movement and healthy creative and sexual expressions. Psychologically, Fire is naturally in motion, catalysing inner light, spirituality and vision. Being an inspirational element, it rises upwards and moves forward, and requires space to expand. Its positive expressions are warming, brightening, uplifting and motivating.

"Suddenly, the whole orchard was ablaze with light, as if the Sun had risen at midnight. It was the Firebird. The Firebird had come, with wings that shone like gold and eyes that gleamed like crystal … (The feather the Firebird left behind) was so glorious that the king immediately forgot about his orchard. The feather was full of brilliance, like a thousand candles all alight at once."
Edited extract from *Prince Ivan and the Firebird*

As illustrated in the passage above, the fiery spark that sets the process of creation going is personified in a number of mythological fiery creatures. The salamander living in the flames in our emblem is one such. Many of them are birds, like the legendary Phoenix, the mighty bird of Fire which arises from the ashes. There is also the Simurgh, bird of Divine Light in Asian mythology, and the Sun-bird of ancient Lycia, which takes souls and flies them up to the sky after death.

The Firebird, a miraculous animal from Russian folklore, as the previous extract outlines, is the bird of inspiration. It has been said its feathers shine as if made from silver and gold and its eyes sparkle like crystals. It sits upon a golden perch and, at midnight, illuminates gardens and fields as brightly as a thousand lights. When the Firebird sings, pearls fall from its break and the sound has the power to heal the sick. It feeds on golden apples which have the power to endow immortality and beauty to those who eat them. A single feather from its tail will light a room; and one feather from her tail is said to be enough to set you off on a Quest. Fire can indeed set us ablaze with enthusiasm. Sometimes it must be seized with both hands, and once the Fire is ignited, it demands action, energy and risk-taking. Fire is not just for the chosen few, for we all have a chance to find a spark and use it; but once discovered, it demands decisive commitment.

According to the I Ching, the hexagram li/li, fire over fire, suggests that, "A luminous thing giving out light must have within itself something that perseveres; otherwise it will burn itself out."

Fire is crucial to alchemy, because heat is a key agent in transformation. Fire also effects colour changes, another critical component of the alchemical process. Further, most of us have some significant memory, fascination, fear, wonder, nervousness or curiosity about fire. Fire can quickly get out of control, and as such careful regulation of it is crucial, both literally and metaphorically in terms of our own enthusiasm. It can destroy, but for all its destruction, it can provide the perfect conditions for the seeds of new life to spring forth. Fire must be controlled however, for enthusiasm is a useful tool but a terrible master, as it drives out discernment and discrimination.

Red, yellow and orange are the colours associated with Fire, and other associations include the Sun, candles, lanterns, swords, warfare, wands, volcanoes, beacons, torches, salamanders, rams, lions, dragons and phoenixes.

Fire comes from the Sun, our great 'Father' in the sky whose warmth and radiance uplifts us all. As followers upon a magical path, we must possess a Fire within us too - a Fire of vision which brings in its wake strong and true wisdom. For when we are carriers of this flame, we can go forth into the world as a beacon of warmth and light.

Positive Fire Qualities ★ Warm, enthusiastic, spirited, idealistic, honest, exuberant, playful, self-motivated, generous, sincere, action-orientated, self-expressive, open, generous, romantic, illuminating, direct, freedom-seeking, optimistic, future-orientated, self-confident, passionate, creative, individualistic, spontaneous, adventurous, pioneering, initiating, inspiring, spiritual, visionary. Fiery temperaments are positive and extroverted, pushing ahead through life with charisma, confidence and buoyancy. They are demonstrative, dramatic, intense and affectionate, with a strong intuitive quality.

Negative Fire Qualities ★ Self-centred, impatient, unrestrained, without boundaries, pushy, careless, reckless, overconfident, insensitive, wilful, self-deluding, volatile, childish, unable or unwilling to reflect, sulky, lacking in perspective, hasty, angry, impractical, thoughtless, forceful, intrusive, restless, immature, driven by desires and sexual urges, egocentric, extravagant, overbearing, melodramatic, imposing, tactless, comes on too strong, temperamental, ungrounded, wild, hyperactive, impulsive, unstable, inconsistent, clumsy, out of touch with own body, and explosive. Fiery temperaments can suffer from 'burnout' through their excessive enthusiasm, energy and impulsivity, and may feel flat or depressed when life deals them a blow.

THE ARCHANGEL OF FIRE ★ MICHAEL

An archangel is an angel of greater than ordinary rank. They possess a stronger, more powerful essence than the guardian angels, through overseeing and guiding the other angels who are said to be with us here on Earth. The word 'angel' derives from the Greek word *angelos* meaning 'messenger'. To humans, angels are often seen as bringers as all sorts of messages. Angels in all their forms are believed to bring the message of 'spirit' into matter, carrying the blueprints of creation and the Source from the Divine into the manifest world. Angels are not and never have been human; they, like fairies and nature spirits, are part of a different evolutionary pattern – but they do appear to us in human form (usually with wings) because that is what we understand. An angel can be in many different places at once, and with the same intensity and concentration, and wish for us to be aware of them and benefit from them.

There are said to be three categories of angels in the cosmos, each with three subdivisions *. 'Angel' is the generic term and also relates specifically to those closest to the physical. Similarly, archangel may be taken to mean any of the higher orders, and indeed signifies the order just above ordinary 'angel'. Found in a number of religious traditions, the word 'archangel' itself is usually associated with the Abrahamic religions. The word archangel is of Greek origin, and means literally 'chief angel'. All archangels end with the 'el' suffix, 'el' meaning 'in God' and the first part of the name meaning what each individual Angel specialises in. The archangel who rules your sign will be the one with whom you most resonate. The astrological sign is an energy signature, a matrix of a specific stellar pattern that will subtly affect and influence you. Although there are many associations for the great archangels of the Universe, we must keep in mind there is great overlapping in their duties and guidance. For example, we may say that one is for healing and another for protection, but they can all perform the functions of the others, and each has only areas of greater focus and responsibilities. Four of the multitude of archangelic beings work intimately with the Earth. These are Raphael (Air), Michael (Fire), Gabriel (Water) and Uriel (Earth). Associated with each of these archangels are one of the four elements, specific colours, one of the four directions or quarters of the Earth, three signs of the zodiac, and a variety of other energies and powers.

Understanding these associations and considering them in relation to our own paths, can help us determine with which of them we are more likely to resonate. Your sign, being of the Fire element, vibrates to the essence of Michael.

* The first sphere, the *Heavenly Counsellors*, comprises Seraphim, Cherubim and Thrones. The second sphere, the *Heavenly Governors*, comprises Dominions, Virtues and Powers. The third sphere, the *Heavenly Messengers*, comprises Principalities, Archangels and Angels. Of course, all such classifications are a human construct, a way of placing order upon the unknowable and allowing us to perceive something about which we have no words to express. However, as long as we think of angelic hierarchies as a way of working with celestials, of remembering important attributes, and we are able to imagine and experience these beings, this order of angels will prove useful to those wishing to draw upon their messages and assistance.

★ ARCHANGEL MICHAEL'S ASSOCIATIONS ★

Element of Fire
The southern quarter of the Earth
The Autumn season
The colour red
The astrological signs of Aries, Leo and Sagittarius

Michael, meaning "Who is like God or the Divine," is the leader of all the archangels and is in charge of courage, truth, strength and integrity. He protects us physically, emotionally and psychically.

Michael helps us to follow our truth without compromising our integrity, and helps us find our true natures so we can be faithful to who we really are. Overall, Michael is the archangel of protection, peace, safety, clarity, balance, and moving forward. This being works to bring patience and a safeguard against any psychic imbalances or dangers. Michael helps us to tear down the old and build the new.

SAGITTARIUS'S ZODIAC ARCHANGEL ★ ZADKIEL

Additionally, each sign is associated with a particular archangel. Such knowledge can help you to build up a relationship with these beings, based upon your strengths and needs. However, no link is rigid, and as you work with angels you will come to develop your own affinities. When invoking a specific archangel, a useful ritual to draw them closer is to light a candle in that angel's colour, burn some oil or incense of its scent, and hold the appropriate crystal while focusing on what you are needing guidance on.

YOUR ARCHANGEL ★ Zadkiel teaches us to trust in the Universe. Labelled 'the holy one', he brings mercy and kindness and aids meditation, brings psychic protection and boosts the immune system. Zadkiel removes emotions and obstacles that are holding you back, so that you are able to see the bigger picture.

SCENT/OIL ★ Cedarwood

CANDLE COLOUR ★ Violet

CRYSTAL ★ Amethyst

THE DEVIC REALMS & FIRE ★ SOUTH: REALM OF THE SALAMANDERS

"Through magick we do conjure the Elements, evoking unto us the special properties of the Life-force for our learning and our coming-into-light. And yet are there secret paths of knowledge that have fallen from the minds of men … For the way of Magick is a path to sacred knowledge, of reverence and humility - and the world is a wondrous place. Yet how many amongst us have fathomed these depths?"
***Merlin's Book of Magick and Enchantment*, Nevill Drury**

Deva is a Sanskrit word that means 'shining one'. Devas are the life force within nature, and there are four devic realms - Fire, Earth, Air and Water - which contain ethereal elemental spirits or sprites. Elementals are the building blocks of nature, and close to being true energy and consciousness. The four elements correspond to four different states of matter: energy/transmutation (Fire), gas (Air), liquid (Water) and solid (Earth), which are linked to the four human states of consciousness: inspiration, thought, feeling and practicality. There are four spirits, or elementals, which reside in the devic realms, associated with each element. People have been painting pictures, telling stories and writing about these devic realms for hundreds of years, albeit sometimes through disguised mediums such as fairytales or children's fantasy stories like Tolkien's *Lord of the Rings*. The power of the natural world is easily observed and since ancient times primal forces have been ascribed to various spirit beings. Belief in nature spirits is of such ancient origin and is Universal; cultures everywhere have names or words to describe them. In the sixteenth century, a famous Swiss physician, alchemist and mystic called Paracelsus * defined these beings as 'Elementals', classifying them according to the element of nature they inhabit. There are four main levels of elemental beings: Gnomes (Earth), Undines (Water), Sylphs (Air), and Salamanders (Fire). The fifth element of Ether is the element from which came forth the other four, and Ether, or Spirit, has never been defined in any particular category, and encompasses the aspects and beings of all the other elements.

Elementals are usually benevolent guardian beings or spirits that look after nature's secrets and treasures in whatever part of the natural realm they occupy. They can only be seen or 'felt' by those possessing heightened psychic abilities, yet they can be summoned by those practising alchemy, spells and magic in order to harness the forces of nature for their own particular intentions. In our modern lives, it may seem as though this magic doesn't exist, but the truth is that most of us are simply less in touch with it than ever before. The consequence of this is that we are destroying vast areas of land, polluting waters, creating toxic landscapes, and disrespecting the laws of nature, which often whisper their messages softly. It is therefore important for us to look at the beauty that surrounds us with true appreciation and genuine regard, and to open ourselves up to the magic resides within it. The four devic realms can teach us much about nature; they act as custodians for the four elements, and learning to work with them is a way of attuning to all the energies and beings of nature. Elementals are four-dimensional, and have nothing to obstruct their movements. Therefore, they move as easily through matter as we do through air and space. They do require some contact with humans for their own evolution. Helping to direct them is an overseer, traditionally called the King of that element, and an archangel. Each of these elements is affiliated with one of the four directions and each elemental spirit embodies its own special energy. If you wish to re-connect and re-harmonise yourself by working with nature and its messages and lessons, you could begin by learning a little about your element's realm: Your element is Fire, which is connected with the South direction and the realm of the Salamanders.

* Paracelsus is considered the most original medical thinker of the sixteenth century. His belief in supernatural beings, intuition and the invisible causes of illness helped him discover hydrogen and nitrogen. Paracelsus believed that "Elementals are unlike pure spirits for they are mortal, but they are not like man for they have no soul."

★ SALAMANDERS ★

These are not to be confused with the reptile salamanders, although they have the same name. Fire spirits are described as thick, red and dry-skinned beings called salamanders, which look similar to the common scaleless lizard-like amphibians that share their name. Elemental salamanders are sometimes visible as small balls of fire and have also been seen in the shape of tongues of flame that can run over fields and peer into dwellings. No fire is lit without their help. In fact, the salamander comes from the Greek word *salambe*, meaning 'fireplace'. These spirits control all manner of flame, lightning, explosions, volcanoes and combustion. Mostly they are active underground and internally within the body and mind. Salamanders evoke powerful emotional currents in humans, and stimulate fires of spiritual idealism and perception. Their energy is much like that of the Tarot Card The Tower, assisting in the tearing down of the old and the building of the new - as fire can be both constructive and destructive in its creative expression.

The salamanders are the guardians of summer and Fire, and reside in the realm of passion, change, prophetic visions, personal power, inspiration and the inner child. They function in the physical body by aiding circulation and in maintaining proper body temperature, and working with the body's metabolism for greater health.

Fire elementals work with humans via heat, fire and flame. This includes everything from the flame of a candle to the ethereal flames and daily light of the Sun. They can be powerfully effective in healing work, but must be used carefully for such applications, as their energies are dynamic and difficult to control. They are almost always present when there is any healing going to occur. Fire provides us with warmth, fuel and heating, and voraciously destroys the old so new life can spring forth out of the ashes - it is the essence from which the legendary phoenix arises. Fire also represents the inner child, that place of innocence from which we all stem. As it gives rise to sexual fervour it is also the root of our creative spirits. The fire elementals can indeed awaken in us higher spiritual visions and aspirations. They strengthen and stimulate the entire auric field to enable easier attunement to and recognition of Divine forces within our lives.

The salamanders can be seen in the heart of fires, dancing like dragons in the flames, and this dragon symbology is used in many Eastern religions to pay homage to them. Salamanders love the Fire for it is nourished by it - yet it is so cold within itself that it cannot be harmed by the flames. They help blacksmiths in their task of forging mighty swords and armour, feeding strength into the flames to have it then yield into the blacksmith's purpose. And yet the salamander is a mighty and tenacious defender of Fire. Only the strongest powers can hold it at bay - it can then be a loyal ally and not an enemy to bar us on our quest. The King of Fire is Belenos or Djin, its archangel is Michael, its magickal tool is the wand (which calls down the spirits into form), and its sacred ceremonial stones are Yellow Topaz, Amber and Citrine.

INVOKING THE FIRE DEVAS

If you wish to increase your sexual prowess, inspiration or creativity, need some career or goal luck, are fearful of an imminent but necessary change or move, or you are in need of courage or energy to meet a challenge, ask the fire devas for their help.

You can encounter salamanders most easily in a bonfire or open hearth. Some see them as sparks or flashes of colour. Dragon-like beings that live within flames, you can see them coiling within the swirling and lapping heat of the flames, and watch others dance and crackle in the sparks. They also reside in every beam of sunlight and flow of electricity. If you do not have access to a proper fire, a candle can serve the same purpose: call upon their help by meditating upon a lit candle. Lighting several at once, particularly in the colours of red and orange, may heighten the power.

THE SOUTH DIRECTION'S CORRESPONDENCES

If you wish to work more with your particular element and direction, the following may help propel your wishes and magical journey:

Time of Day ★ Noon
Polarity ★ Male, negative
Exhortation ★ To dare
Musical Instruments ★ Brass instruments
Colours ★ Scarlet red
Season ★ Summer

Magical Instrument ★ Sword, dagger, athame
Altar Symbol ★ Lamp
Communion Symbol ★ Heat
Archangel ★ Michael
Human Sense ★ Sight
Art Forms ★ Dance, drama
Animals ★ Salamanders, lizards
Mythical Beast ★ Dragon
Magical Arts ★ Ritual
Guide Forms ★ Sun, protector god
Meditation ★ Bonfires
Images & Themes ★ Flames, volcanoes, midday Sun, walking through fire

HOW YOU CAN GET IN TOUCH WITH YOUR FIRE ENERGY

"To be alive is to be burning"

★ Use Fire energy when making wishes around the following: Banishing bad habits, enthusiasm, initiative, inspiration, playfulness, leadership, bringing out the inner child, courage, confidence, dynamic energy, psychic protection, passion and desire

★ In magical practices, Fire can be represented by a candle (red or yellow will strengthen its fiery association), a fireplace, smudge sticks, bonfires or, symbolically, a wand. The candle wax of a burning candle represents Fire's powers of change and transformation - melting as it burns, changing its shape and substance

★ The best days on which to employ Fire magic are Tuesday, ruled by the fiery red planet Mars, or a Sunday, ruled by the blazing Sun. If possible, choose midday when the Sun is at its zenith

★ Eat spicy, hot foods, such as chilli and cayenne, and use fiery spices and sauces

★ Burn a bridge, clean a slate

★ Write your wish/es down on a piece of red paper, then burn it to release the smoke along with its message into the Universe to be fulfilled

★ Spend time in the Sun every day if possible, and around fires of all kinds - stoves, candles, fireplaces, camp fires

★ Yellow and orange-coloured crystals will activate your connection with the element of Fire and enhance your creativity.

★ Practice candle magic

★ Drink green tea

★ Indulge in forms of caffeine such as coffee and chocolate, but do so moderately or you may become jittery, scattered and jumpy, and therefore render your inner Fire ineffective

★ Use supplements which are designed to support and believed to enhance your Fire energy, such as ginger, spirulina and ginseng. Some energy bars may also prove beneficial

★ Practice deep breathing and meditation exercises and disciplines, which help to increase and circulate energy and blood throughout your body

★ Meditate using the Fire mantra "Ram"

★ Indulge in sexual release regularly

★ Schedule and maintain an ongoing physical exercise routine

★ Learn and practice yoga

★ Create a 'Fire ritual', during which you regularly 'burn' away something which needs releasing or banishing

★ Take an acting, drama or theatrics class - or better still, become an actor on camera or on stage!

★ Learn about Fire gods and goddesses, and how they can benefit you. The Hawaiian Fire goddess Pele, is a great place to start

★ Meditate on the Wands suit in the Tarot (the Wands suit represents the Fire element)

★ Express yourself regularly and freely, either through the expressive arts, social events, or even a journal

★ Be bold, brave and courageous, even when you are not feeling like it

★ Choose a challenge and rise to it

★ Build your confidence daily by listing three achievements or goals you have reached, no matter how seemingly small or large

★ Wear and surround yourself with the colours red and orange

★ Commit yourself to a bright future by creating a vision or dream, and maintain it by keeping track of your steps along the way

★ Think and act big. As Marianne Williamson said: "Our deepest fear is not that we are inadequate. Our deepest fear is that we are powerful beyond measure. It is our light, not our darkness, that most frightens us. Your playing small does not serve the world … We are all meant to shine as children do … And as we let our own lights shine, we unconsciously give other people permission to do the same." So be bold and shine!

★ When working with the Fire element in magical practice, stand at the South quarter of your magical space, as the South is its domain, and invite its living essence into your circle or space

★ Fire spirits are known by metaphysicians as salamanders, and they inspire passion, blessings, new life, creativity, and spiritual healing. With all this in mind, Fire signs would be wise to adopt one as their very own spirit guide!

YOUR MODE ★ MUTABLE

Each sign belongs to one of the three quadruplicities, Cardinal, Fixed and Mutable. If we closely examine the Earth's yearly cycle, we can form a very accurate picture of the nature of these quadruplicities, for they correspond directly with the manifestation of the seasons. Each season has three months: the first month brings the new phase of the cycle, the second month brings a concentration of the season's energy to its fullest expression, and the third month represents the transition from the current season to the next one. The astrological quadruplicities represent the three basic qualities in all life: creation (Cardinal), perseveration (Fixed) and destruction (Mutable). Every thing that is born, from a period of time to a human being, experiences a life and then dies. In this context, death can be taken to mean that the form of the energy changes; but the energy itself can never be annihilated, for form is mortal, whereas essence is immortal.

The Mutable mode covers the signs Gemini, Virgo, Sagittarius and Pisces, and is the most flexible group of the three modes (the others being Cardinal and Fixed), able to shift and change to facilitate action. You instinctively know how to go with the flow and you adapt most easily to new situations and have diverse interests, but can lack perseverance and are prone to restlessness. Operating with flexibility and mobility, you are adaptable to change and have a circulating quality. Cooperative and friendly, you can fit in almost anywhere, put up with anything and turn any situation to your advantage. You can steer projects through periods of transition and can also bring them to a conclusion, but are conspicuously absent when hard work, long hours or persistent effort is necessary (with the exception of Virgo). Although gentle, generally easy going and likeable, you can be childish, sulky and ruthless if threatened. And although you have a natural benevolent streak and love to help animals and people, you can also be paradoxically selfish. The natural versatility of the Mutable quadruplicity can develop into a willingness to change and compromise, which gives an enormous sense of resourcefulness to these signs. Being so versatile, you are constantly seeking ways you can make improvements to yourself and your life; Mutable signs can always be relied upon to think of new and ingenious ways of dealing with changing circumstances. However, without the proper focus, centralising force, direction or persistence, your energy can become easily scattered, flighty, wavering and disoriented - and thus ultimately ineffective. You often lack a fixity and determination of purpose, which are needed to concretise goals. Your essential energy is one of movement, flow, fluidity, adaptability, adjustability, harmony, and versatility. Your feelings can switch and shift easily and you can be moody, indecisive, inconsistent and unpredictable. And although resourceful and ingenious, you can often project nervousness and worry. You may act as the intermediate between the Cardinal and Fixed signs. Mutable also indicates the ending of seasons, which are times of change and transition, merging into new territories and changing conditions.

Sagittarius is the most expansive and broad-minded of the Mutable quality; you seek the truth above all else and you constantly adapt as your knowledge increases. You are personable and diplomatic and like to treat everyone equally and fairly, albeit inconsistently. Strongly ethical, your morals may also change to suit your surroundings and circumstances.

YOUR RULING PLANET ★ JUPITER

The Great Benefic, Expander & Bringer of Joy

Planetary Meditation
I am my Earth (my body),
and my Sky (my transcendence)
I am my Sun (my spirit),
and my Moon (my soul)
I am my Venus (my pleasure),
and my Jupiter (my faith)
I am my Mars (my courage),
and my Saturn (my lessons)
I am my Mercury (my thoughts),
and my Uranus (my truth)
I am my Neptune (my dreams),
and my Pluto (my transformation)

Each planet has its own distinctive and original meaning which, according to its position in the zodiac, combines with the qualities that are inherent in each of the twelve astrological signs. If a planet is your sign's ruler, however, it exerts a significant influence upon your life, regardless of its birth chart or zodiacal position.

Benefic ★ Associated with Expansion, Religion, Faith, Philosophy, Higher Education, Travel ★ 11.9 Year Cycle

★ KEY WORDS ★

Expansion, Wisdom, Travel, Abundance, Faith, Ethics, Morals, Ideals, Distant Horizons, Inflation, Culture, Philosophy, Beliefs, Knowledge, Enthusiasm, Religion, Luck, Fortune, Trust, Hope, Vision, Justice, Opportunities, Joy, Benevolence, Optimism, Exploration, Education, Success, Wellbeing, Confidence, Indulgence, Creative Visualisation, Opulence, Conscience, Betterment, Extravagance, Generosity

★ KEY CONCEPTS ★

★ Exploration of New & Foreign Places ★
★ Belief, Philosophy, Theology & Religion ★
★ Morals, Ethics, Truth, Laws & Justice ★
★ Higher Education ★
★ Understanding of Universal Laws Governing Humanity ★
★ Expansion on the Spiritual, Mental & Physical Levels ★
★ Luck, Expansion & Opportunities ★
★ Publishing & Legal Matters ★
★ Large Animals & the Great Outdoors ★
★ Gambling, Risk & Speculation ★

Day ★ Thursday

Number ★ 3

Basic Energy & Magic ★ Expansion, Faith, Philosophy

Colour ★ Purple, Deep Blue, Indigo

Gods/Goddesses/Angel ★ Zeus, Jupiter, Sachiel

Metals ★ Tin, antimony

Gems/Minerals ★ Amethyst, Lapis Lazuli, Topaz, Turquoise

Trees/Shrubs ★ Oak, Cedar, Ash, Birch, Linden, Chestnut

Flowers/Herbs ★ Sweet William, Sage, Nutmeg

Woods ★ Oak, Cedar

Fabric ★ Velvet

Animals ★ Horse, Eagle

Element ★ Fire

Zodiacal Signs ★ Sagittarius, Pisces

Zodiacal Influences ★ Rules Sagittarius, Co-rules Pisces; Exalted in Cancer; Detriment Gemini; Fall Capricorn

A giant planet shrouded in swirling cloud, Jupiter was considered the beneficent father of the gods by many ancient cultures. Jupiter is the largest planet orbiting the Sun, and is bigger than all the other planets in our Solar system combined. The wonder of its size can be imagined when we consider that it is approximately 800 million kilometres away from the Sun, and can still be viewed in the sky as our second brightest planet (after Venus). The vast 'empty' space between its nearest neighbour, Mars, and Jupiter, is almost as inconceivable - 550 million kilometres - and is littered with cosmic rubble; this space is otherwise known as the 'asteroid belt'.

In mythology, the Roman god Jupiter, Zeus to the Greeks, the Nordic Thor, and parallel deities in other cultures, sometimes appears more powerful than even the Sun gods, hinting at Jupiter's mighty influence. Wisdom, learning and justice were their attributes, thunder and lightning their visible power; Jupiter was called the Thunderer and his chief weapon was the thunderbolt. Zeus, who sat upon his throne atop his holy mountain with a thunderbolt in one hand and the staff of wisdom and life in the other, was seen as a combined Divine package of creator (the staff), preserver (the mountain), and destroyer (the lightning bolt). Known as a 'cloud gatherer', and sky and weather god in more ancient incarnations, sacred to Jupiter were the oak *, the eagle and mountain summits. He was the omnipotent ruler of the ancient Greek gods who lived on the summit of Mount Olympus, and was regarded as the father of men and possibly even the master of *fate*. The Romans considered him the guardian of the law, protector of justice and virtue, and defender of the truth, hence Jupiter's long-held associations with these concepts.

Jupiter is the second largest planet and for much of the time the second brightest planet in the sky, shining creamy white. Jupiter is visible for substantial and continuous amounts of time. Jupiter, also known as the Sky Father, was the supreme Roman god, ruler of the Universe. Like his Greek counterpart Zeus, he controlled thunderbolts, which were said to be carried by eagles, monarchs of the bird kingdom.

In astrology, Jupiter is the first of the transpersonal planets, which is less associated with the self and more concerned with interactions between ourselves - in other words, it can be classified as a 'social planet'. Regarded as the most benevolent and wise of the planets, Jupiter is the joy-bringer and is related to expansion in every form, the acquisition of knowledge, and the desire to be free and unrestrained. In its purest sense, Jupiter encompasses morals, altruism, good fortune, prosperity, higher values, ethics, beliefs, exploration, spiritual leanings, aspirations, ideals, faith, hope and trust.

Buoyantly optimistic, Jupiter's main function is to grow and exaggerate everything he touches. However, he inflates and expands indiscriminately, often making bad points worse and good points better. He not only brings material benefits, but is also the source of philosophical wisdom. He imparts this knowledge frequently by coming to the rescue at the last minute, when all hope seems lost. Saturn is also a wise teacher, but teaches through restriction, limitations and adversity, without any immediately apparent saving graces. Jupiter's very nature is to fulfil - he delivers the goods at the end of the lesson. At his best, he can be the happy ending, and the strength that allows us to endure trials. But Jupiter's blind enthusiasm can just as easily lead to fanaticism as his enjoyment of pleasures can lead to perilous excesses.

Jupiter is the largest planet of the Solar system. It determines how outward looking, expansive (or constrictive) and broad-minded we are. It can govern how we express our happiness in life and how we relate to and enjoy the abundance, joy and material luxuries of our worlds. It is a planet which influences lifestyle - namely, excess and indulgence. Through his powerful influence, we may become an extremist, or excessive optimism and carelessness can mar our judgement; similarly, losses are likely through ill-judged investments, gambling and extravagance. The other danger in Jupiter's benevolence is that you may fail to see or take full advantage of opportunities. In essence, Jupiter often doesn't know when to stop, and is always the last to leave the party - and then go straight to another!

Even the symbol of this jumbo planet is optimistic - the Moon-like half circle of soul rises slightly above the cross of matter and suggests a higher wisdom and mastery over material things. This glyph (or symbol) for Jupiter, the cross of matter with an upright semi-circle or crescent of consciousness, attached to the left arm, symbolises its beginnings on the Earthly plane leading upwards to new levels of awareness. However, the crescent faces inwards and can be taken to signify either inner enlightenment *or* self-orientation and indulgence.

Broad-visioned and future-oriented, Jupiter paints a big picture and impels you to think, act and dream large. Jupiter brings hope, honesty, spirituality and fortuity to the birth chart, expanding and creating opportunities in whichever area of the chart it is found. Where he exists in your chart, you will find special opportunities for progress. You will observe clues to furthering your career, to broadening your relationships with the material world, and chances to heighten your spirituality. You will see ways to make money or to acquire skills to help you get what you want. But always bear in mind that the slip side of Jupiter's coin is that he reveals those areas of life in which we may be drawn to adverse excesses or blind adherences.

Jupiter has much to tell us about our urge for expansion, and the types of physical and mental travel, opportunities, justice, religious viewpoints and philosophical wisdom we undertake and express. His energy is philosophising, and as such is deeply connected with our search for meaning in life. Largely to do with morals, ethics, beliefs and ideals, it describes the means by which we grow and ultimately find that meaning. Linked with conscience, his urge for growth is part of our human need for mystical experiences. This sense and feeling, that there is something beyond human knowledge and existence encourages our exploration into deeper meanings, which is one of Jupiter's very functions. A well-placed Jupiter in our birth chart supports a developed sense of moral values and a philosophical approach to living. This positive side of Jupiter increases wisdom so that our primitive desire to look after the basic needs of the self is sacrificed in order to serve the interests of other human beings, or at the very least, our personal social sphere.

Jupiter is linked with prosperity, wealth, luck, and good fortune, as well as our faith, hope, trust and optimism in a bright future. As Jupiter expands everything with which it comes into contact, and rules tangible, solid financial gains, it is the giver of gifts and luck. Finding one's higher purpose, or inner riches, is also considered a pervasive Jupiter influence. This massive, boundless, dense ball of gas, encourages the creation and exchange of ideas across all cultures, nations, colours, races, and even timelines.

Jupiter is a social planet, which tells us much about our urge for higher learning and long distance travel, particularly of the variety which exposes us to other people and new ideas. It tells us about our philosophical outlook on life, our point of attraction for luck, joy and abundance, and as such is our own personal lucky guide. Jupiter signifies the modes by which we both physically and mentally travel. Jupiter's influence enhances our creative visualisation skills, holding them in the vortex of creation and manifestation. Its essence is what lies at the heart of making one's own luck: if you can visualise something with enough passion, intensity and faith, you can seize the chance when it arises to make what you want *happen*. In this sense, Jupiter is all about seizing the day!

In our birth chart, the Sun and Jupiter both exercise the kingly function of harnessing vital energies for the purpose of conscious achievement and personal growth. And indeed, both planets participate in the expressions of male archetype in all of us. The Sun and Jupiter are quite different planets, however. Jupiter has often been described as a social planet, whereas the Sun is termed a personal planet and, along with the Moon, the *most* personal of planets. Furthermore, the Sun is considered a spiritual influence, while Jupiter a more temporal force, a distinction which may be difficult to understand for the uninitiated. Jupiter has been integrally linked to the Sun in mythology, religion - and astrology, and in ancient Greece and Rome, Jupiter was assigned an even higher position that its Solar counterpart.

The Sun can bring each individual's vital force under his personal control, and this focusing of power gives us a sense of direction. It can orient us towards business, learning, relationships, or spirituality - any number of possible goals. How we extend that energy into the world, how this directed energy functions in the social sphere, is the question we must ask Jupiter, for these are Jupiter's role and domain. With Jupiter, our directed will is focused on social goals and growth, luck and general expansion in whatever area of life we wish to grow. The important questions to ask our chart's Jupiter is what kind of attitudes do we bring to our goals? And what kind of spirit do we embody during our quest for success? These wise inner kings, the Sun and Jupiter, organise and focus the entire range of our psycho-spiritual energy and directs it to a specific purpose, while the Warrior (Mars) lends the motivation and drive to do the actual work.

While the Sun may be regarded as the essential core of our being which directs us towards our true spiritual goal, it is through Jupiter that we make our goals *real* in a worldly sense. If it weren't for this expansive planet, our dreams may well stay within our core and feed our essence, but not necessarily be *achieved* or realised. Jupiter's optimism and striving helps bring them out.

Especially in esoteric astrology, Jupiter has been described as the protector or 'inner guide' of the natal chart. For example, a Sixth House Jupiter may protect our health, while a Twelfth House Jupiter may offer spiritual protection. Its place in our horoscope is where it bestows upon us gifts; and it also represents our own capacity for generosity, particularly if placed in a warm or giving sign or house.

Indeed, this kingly planet impels us to walk in the world with a benevolent spirit and sincere generosity. However, it does has its drawbacks, and there is such a thing as excess and *too much* abundance. These excesses of lifestyle or thinking, may manifest as a weight problem, extreme or overbearing behaviour, or an inflated sense of self-confidence or entitlement. It may lead to a certain arrogance or smugness, or to a condition of static complacency. In combination with Venus and/or Neptune, it may increase tendencies towards hedonism, or indulgence in sex, alcohol, drugs or food.

Jupiter has always been the signification of good fortune, spiritual faith, good fellowship and joy; another name for the God in Latin was 'Jove', from which where the word 'jovial' derives.

The position of Jupiter at the moment of your birth determines your potential for growth and expansion on many levels, including physical, intellectual and spiritual growth. It also describes where and how you will accumulate material assets, power and status. Jupiter shows in which areas of your life you have faith, optimism and good luck; it represents the level of confidence you have and how you can grow and be fulfilled. It also shows your higher levels of thinking and your views on issues such as religion, spirituality, philosophy and social issues. In its more negative expression, Jupiter unveils aspects of your character where you have a tendency to be irresponsible, reckless or overindulgent, and it reveals any unrealistic expectations - in other words, upon which areas of life you focus any over-idealism.

Knowing all this about Jupiter, it is perhaps not so coincidental that Sagittarius, ruled by Jupiter, falls in the part of the year between Thanksgiving and Christmas, a time of year that is imbued with the Jupiterian activities of exchanging gifts and offerings, indulging in large spreads of food and drinks, engaging in social merriment, and the gathering together of family and friends from far and wide to celebrate the spirit of the season.

Overall, Jupiter's most noble gift is to guide you to your highest happiness and fulfilment. As the planet of increase and growth, some of its pathways are through challenges, temptations, learning and travel. Jupiter in your chart drops clues about where and how to take leaps of faith. The essence of Jupiter is expansion to accommodate for absorption. Jupiter symbolises the energy within ourselves that magnifies our psyche and opens it up to attract and absorb opportunity and luck, and its function is to utilise the wisdom gained from living and digesting an array of experiences. Having an optimistic and positive energy, Jupiter sees our mistakes as opportunities rather than failure. It is intuitive rather than analysing in its devising of meaningful answers, selectively dismissing something if it is meaningless. While Mercury is interested in gossip, Jupiter judges it as good or bad and moves in or moves on accordingly.

Mercury is concerned with mentality in a pure and simple sense, while Jupiter gives the ability to think ahead, to understand the ramifications of your thought processes, to appreciate long-term significance and purpose; in other words, Jupiter will assist you to find meaning and direction. Also, Jupiter in your birth chart will show the nature of your belief systems - what you find meaningful - and the measure of your faith (this of course, does not necessarily relate to organised religion, but rather our adherence to personal creeds, moral standards and sets of principles). Jupiter goes beyond the rational faculties embodied by Mercury, and gives the gift of prophecy, while Mercury chooses the mode of expression and words in which Divine revelations are to be imparted. Mercury informs how people can communicate with other people, while Jupiter tells how people can communicate with gods and higher powers. Jupiter is very strongly associated with principles and matters on a higher plane. Its inflationary nature allows you to see the big picture by widening and opening up your horizons. The combination of this vision with thought, leads to the attainment of Jupiter's loftiest aim: *wisdom*.

Jupiter spends approximately one year in each zodiac sign, completing a full cycle every twelve years. Its oppositions and returns are the most significant milestones of its cycle, and one of these will occur every six years of our lives, beginning at the age of six. If transiting Jupiter conjuncts, or aligns with, your natal Jupiter (every 12 years), you have an increased chance of having a lucky break, receiving a windfall, or experiencing something that advances and expands you in mind, body or spirit.

In essence, Jupiter is abundance personified, and because Jupiter also represents righteousness and philosophical dominion, we may decide to act upon what we believe to be right and therefore feel spiritually rewarded by his awesome influence.

Wherever Jupiter is placed in your chart, and the sign it is travelling through at the moment of your birth, will have a significant bearing on your life's lucky path. No matter which house or sign it concerns, it will always bring the opportunity for growth and abundance, inwardly and outwardly. By knowing which sign and which area of life this abundance is likely to manifest, you will be equipped with a higher understanding and knowledge of how to go about opening up to and receiving it more fully into your experience.

Jupiter, the supreme God in the Roman pantheon, tells us of our need for expansion, abundance and wisdom. It is concerned with what we believe in and the philosophies that colour our lives. Jupiter is connected to growth and learning and blesses both our material and spiritual endeavours. Traditionally referred to as the 'greater benefic', people with a prominent Jupiter in their chart possess good judgement and wisdom, are leaders, generous, extravagant, philanthropic, flashy and generally lucky. Too much Jupiterian influence, however, can lead to over-optimism, compulsive behaviours, over-indulgence, excessive risk-taking, carelessness, irresponsibility, arrogance, and being too big for one's boots.

Jupiter is associated with money, law, trust, gains, affluence, sincerity, wealth, morals, international affairs, juries, maximum, excesses, faith, judges, extensions, truth, prosperity, fun, gallantry, exaggeration, surplus, luck, benefactors, titles, explorations, medals, praise, tributes, viscounts, increase, generosity, quantity, leases, the liver, growth, cathedrals, advantages, happiness, hips, travels, humour, holidays, rosaries, honesty, expensive, swelling, hope, missionaries, optimism, bounty, opulence, banks, ordainment, profits, attorneys, winnings, expansion, joviality, legal affairs, faraway places, passports, racehorses, literature, philanthropists, cheer, archery, church, thunder, colleges, convents, animals, copyright, barristers, countries, loans, courts of law, deputies, pilgrims, donations, philosophy, bonuses, plenty, abundance, religion, embassies, good fortune, thighs, endowments, carnivals, enlargement, ethics, books, excellence, finance, worship, aldermen, alderwomen, amplification, awards, mirth, prayer, preachers, goodwill, prizes, quality, blessings, ceremonies, bishops, charity, education (higher), extravagance, foreign affairs, improvement, journeys, judicial system, licences, millionaires, riches, theology, Thursday, tin, trials (law), universities, valuers and accumulation. I'm sure you get the idea!

Overall, if Jupiter's energy is tempered and not allowed to get out of control, you will learn through this enormous mass that it is with patience and maturity that the narrow, everyday path becomes the wide open road to fulfilment, meaning, spirituality and wisdom. The force is there, waiting to be tapped.

In itself, Jupiter's expansive influence is neither beneficial nor harmful, for what it does for us depends on how we channel it.

This Jupiterian energy and influence, throughout your whole life, gives Sagittarians the gifts of generosity, philanthropy, flashiness, extravagance, liveliness, exuberance, and a happy-go-lucky attitude. But too little or a weak Jupiterian influence can indicate someone who is down on their luck, rigid in their expansion, stuck in a rut, pessimistic, makes unlucky decisions, experiences lack often, and attracts general ill fortune. Acknowledging a Jupiterian lack or weakness in the chart can be helpful though, as can working positively with its energies to give its potential a boost. But the Sagittarian needn't worry about this, as just being born under the auspice of the Centaur's domain renders you lucky from the word go; after all, your motto is "I Aim" - and wherever you decide to direct your arrow, it uncannily always seems to hit exactly the mark you were aiming for. How will *you* use your phenomenally powerful Jupiterian influence?

* The oak, or the 'lightning tree' as it is sometimes called, is one of Jupiter's holy trees. Supposedly struck more times by lightning than any other tree, the oak conducts Jupiter's energies to the Earth through its roots. The rustling of oak leaves was once said to be Jupiter's voice. (Also, see under '*Your Lucky Wood*'.)

YOUR HOUSE IN THE HOROSCOPE ★ THE NINTH HOUSE

The Ninth House is connected with thinking and ideas, and how they are applied as organised schemes of thought in wider society. Religion, higher learning, the law, justice, philosophy, personal freedom and travel to broaden the mind also feature here.

A house is one of the twelve sections dividing the terrestrial globe, viewed from a precise time and geographical place, into sectors from the poles to the horizon. The horoscope, or birth chart, is divided into these twelve sections called houses. Each house governs a different area or 'department' of life, such as relationships, career, leisure and even karma. The reason for this division of the Earth into houses can be understood when we consider that the Sun's rays affect us differently in the morning, at noon and at night, and also in summer and winter, and if we study the cause, we will readily observe that it is the angle at which the ray strikes us or the Earth which produces that difference in effect. Similarly, with the stellar rays, astrologers have observed that a child born at or near midday, when the Sun's rays strike the birthplace from the Tenth House, has an improved chance of public or career advancement in life than one born after sunset. By similar observations and tabulations, it has been found that the other planetary rays affect the various departments of life when their ray is projected through the other houses, and therefore each house is said to 'rule' or govern certain departments of the human life experience.

The Ninth House, ruled by Sagittarius, is the house of philosophy, higher education, travel and religion. The gesture of the Archer shooting unveils the meaning of this house, which astrology further describes as the realm of abstract thinking, dreams, visions, and the higher mind and spirit. "A man's reach should exceed his grasp, or what's a Heaven for?" is what Sagittarius ultimately wants to know. It is through his native house that he will search for - and hopefully uncover - the answers to his many questions. This domain is where we outreach our physical and mental embrace of what we know as reality, and aspire toward that which we can sense but cannot see. It is here that we formulate into creeds and philosophical systems the thoughts which the preceding sign Scorpio fished out of the hidden depths.

As a house which is strongly connected with ethics, philosophical thoughts, viewpoints and morals, this house allows for judgement regarding your intellectual and moral qualities, and states whether or not you have a propensity for travel, particularly extensively or to foreign lands. It can also indicate whether changes of locations are desired.

After the complex, transformative and deeply psychological influence of the Eighth House, the Ninth House is like a refreshing, uplifting breeze that blows the cobwebs away through the winds of enlightenment. If the lessons from the Eighth House have been properly learned, we will emerge a little wiser and more evolved, and substantially further forward along the path of life. The Ninth House is where we reach out to something greater, and where Universal truths are explored.

Overseas affairs, higher learning, conscience, freedom, large open spaces and big animals, sports, dreams, adventure, visions, ideals, dogma, culture, doctrine, spirituality, truths, faith, wisdom, the higher mind, moral and legal concerns, the communication of ideas, the study in depth of profound subjects, mental exploration, foreign languages, and other intellectual matters such as religion, science and philosophy are also governed by the Ninth House. It is concerned with how you understand the world and how you conduct your search for deeper meaning and purpose. It shows the way in which you seek to expand your personal horizons, your interactions and relationships with other cultures and distant relatives, and your attitudes and points of view on *all* topics.

The Third House, the opposite of the Ninth House in the horoscope, enables us to gather facts and pieces of information, while the Ninth House synthesises these into a whole and gives them greater significance and meaning. The Ninth House provides spiritual guidance, and shapes our principles and belief systems, encouraging us to see the bigger picture, the broader plan, and our life's overall purpose, essence and direction.

The Ninth House is linked with higher learning and travel. It is often called the area of the higher mind because it is connected with literature, law, philosophy, scientific thought, religion, higher education and anything else which broadens the mind, expands the conscious awareness and widens your mental and physical horizons. As such, it covers academic subjects, law, publishing, athleticism, and long distance and overseas movement. Other exoteric and esoteric keywords include: Intellectual matters, distant journeys (of the mind, body or spirit), cultural learning, the journey along the Path, ageless and timeless wisdom, our spiritual leanings, our philosophies, belief systems, world views, ideals and dreams, and our ultimate search for meaning.

It also indicates any emphasis on morals (noble or corrupt), faith and religion (both usually with strong leanings one way or another), and ethics (honest or dishonest; pure or contaminated), depending on the planets, signs and aspects of this house. Overall, planets and signs placed in the Ninth House illustrate your response to the call of your spirit to higher places.

YOUR OPPOSITE SIGN ★ GEMINI
WHAT YOU CAN LEARN FROM THE TWINS

If we look at the zodiac, we can see that it can be broadly divided into two hemispheres, this division being based on the natural division of the year by the two equinoxes. Astrologers often refer to the first six signs, the hemisphere in which the day predominates (the days being longer in the spring and summer months), as the Personal Sphere of Experience, and the second six signs, the hemisphere in which nights are longer, as the Social Sphere of Experience. These two halves of the zodiac perfectly balance and complement each other, and each individual 'personal' zodiac sign has something to teach its directly opposite 'social' zodiac sign. To generalise, the signs of the personal sphere tend to experience life through a type of self-projection and self-interest which is often socially uncomplicated, unsophisticated or naïve. Their objective is to learn greater social awareness and thereby integrate themselves with the larger, more Universal human collective. On the other hand, the signs of the social sphere are prone to experience life through the use of their more developed social consciousness. In essence, the personal signs (Aries, Taurus, Gemini, Cancer, Leo, Virgo) usually provide stimulation and new energy to their environment, while the social, more Universal signs (Libra, Scorpio, Sagittarius, Capricorn, Aquarius, Pisces) provide experience, opportunities for wider expression, and give a more broad-minded approach and perspective to their surroundings.

Each sign in a pair seeks and is attracted to the qualities of its complementary opposing sign. Gemini seeks to develop the breadth of vision and philosophical outlook embodied by Sagittarius, while Sagittarius wishes for the alacrity and methodology of Gemini. Gemini dwells within the realm of the distribution of *individual* concepts and ideas, while Sagittarius resides within the sphere of the distribution of *social* concepts and ideas.

Although the word 'opposite' conjures up feelings of separateness and differences, the astrological polarities should not be seen as two signs in conflict with each other - their positive expression is to create a natural balance and equilibrium. Each sign has something to learn from its opposite, but also has a contribution to make towards the other sign's more evolved expression. The Third (Gemini) and Ninth (Sagittarius) House polarity is concerned with the immediate environment versus expanded horizons. In fact, the Ninth House is an extension or expansion on the Third House in almost every way: short-distance travel - long-distance travel; early education - higher and further education; direct communication and information - deeper philosophies and exploration; *gathering* information and facts - *seeking meaning in* information and facts. The two balance each other, because the practical immediacy of communication indicated by the Third House is needed if the deeper Ninth House ideas are to be understood.

Positive and Mutable, this polarity is concerned with the mind, and knowledge and how it is acquired and expressed. Gemini is preoccupied with knowledge. Facts are a fascination for Gemini and indeed they are experts at gathering them. But facts without any cohesion are pretty much useless, and Sagittarius can teach Gemini how to see the bigger picture and put them into a much more meaningful *whole*. Sagittarius can bring the height of wisdom to this vast storehouse of often indiscriminately-collected information, allowing the whole picture to be seen more broadly and understood intuitively. Jupiter is the higher octave of Mercury, and yet Gemini can conversely help Sagittarius by bringing the ideals and visions down into the real, practical world of everyday life. Communication is a two-sided process and Gemini can sift information so that it is easily assimilated by other members of the human community.

Sagittarius relates to openness, honesty and learning to trust one's intuition. But it also relates to the failure to listen to others, the preaching of ideals, and believing one is always right. The Gemini, in all his fickleness and simple childlike innocence, can help you to overcome these oft disabling traits.

The Sagittarian follows a different pattern of thinking to Gemini, standing out by his convictions, which are his own, formed from long, profound searches for the truth, which is extracted from many sources. Essentially, the Sagittarius spirit will seek to expand his geographical, intellectual, psychological and spiritual horizons based upon these findings. From the much more trivial, here-and-now Twins, Sagittarius can learn to skim the surface occasionally without indulging the incessant need to burrow deep into *everything* to find its more down-reaching meaning. Not everything needs to have meaning; some things just *are*. Learn from Gemini's humble acceptance of things at face value and you may find your life a little simpler. Although Gemini, through his sheer lack of decisiveness, can often feel overwhelmed by decisions, have too many pots on the boil, too many balls in the air, and a myriad of inner identities fighting for a voice within, his scatterbrained approach can still impart much wisdom. His youthful vigour and uncomplicated mentality is like a refreshingly cool drink from a sparkling spring for the Sagittarian soul.

Way down, deep inside, Sagittarians are accustomed to being totally free. Even though this basic attitude is largely subconscious, it may still be difficult for you to accept all the restrictive and confining duties, obligations and expectations that are part and parcel of everyday life. You would much prefer to be like an untamed brumby, wild and roaming, cantering happily with tossing head and unruly mane, going wherever the wind takes you. But your soul's purpose is calling you to a *lower* plane - not a subordinate one - just earthlier. You have spent long enough roaming the wild, it is now time to learn from your complementary opposite Gemini and tend to the nitty gritty everyday realities of life. As much as you love adventure and freedom, you need to learn how to contain all that raw, primal and vital energy which has propelled you for most of your life, and focus it in ways that first of all teach you, then others, and that also link people together - at ground level. Forget the lofty, out-of-reach zones you have grown accustomed to, ignore the eternal quest for those spiritual pots of gold at the end of the rainbow; it is time to buckle into your saddle and take a more ordinary garden-variety carpet ride which will bring you back down to a more workable level.

Your ideals and philosophies have been largely residing in the clouds until now, but Gemini can teach you how to bring those ideals and philosophies down to a more tangible level and actually *apply* them. Although specialising in trivialities rather than the bigger picture, Gemini can wisely advise that most ideas have their origins in mundane trivia. You need to go back to the beginning and adopt a more innocent, childlike approach to your thinking, in order to - perhaps paradoxically - evolve.

The Twins are the master networkers and can impart the wisdom to you that no man is an island, and that you indeed need to link in with other like-minded souls in order for your outlook to be broadened. Sagittarius, being the eternal freedom-seeker, has grown quite used to living on his own island. Although immeasurably fond of people, his mind often soars a little above everyone else's, not in a condescending way of course, it's just that the Archer likes to idealise his way through life, explaining away everything from the colours of the rainbow to the age-old chicken and egg dilemma. Gemini is adept at gathering the facts, Sagittarius at formulating ideas from them. No sooner have the Twins shared their vast factual bank of thoughts and countless little pieces of information, than they are off, skipping in the other direction, whistling a sweet tune, having completely forgotten everything they have just learned. While Sagittarius can teach Gemini how to see the bigger picture, Gemini can teach Sagittarius to break it down into small bite-sized nuggets.

In many ways, the Tarot card The Fool symbolises the dynamics inherent in this axis. A youngish person, in androgynous clothing, swag hanging from a staff over the shoulder, a dog yapping at the heels, stands at the edge of a precipice, looking towards the sky with a beaming smile. This card is known as the zero card (or first) of the deck by some, and the number twenty-two (or last) by others. The figure zero symbolises unlimited, but unmanifested, potential, while twenty-two stands for the completion of every realm of human experience that the Tarot represents. It embodies quite an apt analogy: from zero to everything; from foolish youth to masterful, wise sage. Like The Fool and his bundle which is said to contain all knowledge, through the possession of this knowledge, you too have the keys to the great meaning and richness of life itself. Whether you are the naïve character about to take his first steps into the wider world (Gemini) or the highly evolved magi-wizard (Sagittarius), both can transmit their lessons through this nodal axis to each other - and both can learn equally important lessons from each other.

If you are a typical Sagittarius, you are likely to be at the higher end of the mental spectrum, but Gemini's youthful, more superficial naiveté can be a refreshing change for you. An essential task on your journey is to round off your innate philosophy, wisdom, belief systems and understanding, and apply them on a purely *human* level, so that you can help others in your wider social circle. You are so used to applying things with your mind on an intangible, spiritual level, that it doesn't translate effectively into your relationships or the wider human experience of which you are a part. Gemini has some great lessons to teach in this realm, for the Twins are truly existent in each and every moment. While your mind is off wandering some distant horizon, planet or time-zone, Gemini is smelling the grass and feeling the wind in his hair in the *here* and *now*. The Archer can learn from this immediacy, for it is in the here and now that things actually get done.

More than a few of you on this axis have to think your way through the decision of whether to live a city or country life at least once in your life. But whatever is decided, you should also take a look at formalising your knowledge through education - university or other studies, for if you buckle down and get on with it - down here on Earth - the results will truly astound you.

Although the Archer has the amazing ability to make the Divine intelligible through the written and spoken word, and the capacity to communicate a meaningful understanding of the bigger picture, sometimes you need to speak in a language that is much clearer, more accessible and less foreign to others.

You often err through impatience or an exacerbated or constant desire to expand, making you further agitated or overly ambitious. This incites you, despite yourself, to dream of far-off places to which you can escape, therefore getting away from responsibilities, as well as social, material and relational obligations. You may also find it difficult to communicate, to listen, or quite simply to enter into conversation with someone. The Twins can encourage you to become more civilised, in other words more *aware* of others, and to put a greater emphasis on human contacts and exchanges in all areas. If you know how to effectively exploit your human, spiritual and intellectual qualities, then you will be able to more fully convey these to those close to you, thereby becoming one step closer to being completely fulfilled.

WHAT THE TWINS CAN ULTIMATELY TEACH THE ARCHER

Release ★ Insatiable desire for expansion, unshakable convictions, escapism, lack of direction, intransigence, agitation, impatience, over-idealism, dwelling in the future

Embrace ★ Curiosity, awareness of others' ideas, flexibility, reality, everyday matters, the little things that give pleasure, trivia, being in the here and *now*

Gemini lives in the present, focuses on immediate realities, gains information, collects data, makes connections, is concerned with facts and figures, thinks inductively (particular to general), emphasises reason, enjoys everyday conversations and small talk, associates with diverse people, is unconcerned with ethical implications, pursues many unrelated interests, possesses many skills, and is amoral, versatile, logical, rational, observant, scientific, empirical, knowledgeable, scattered, restless and interactive.

To evolve to your fullest potential, Gemini teaches you to embrace living in the current moment, not in a distant future; to smell the roses rather than philosophising about them; to express yourself more clearly, openly and unambiguously; to abandon lofty ideals in favour of simplicity; to break the bigger picture down into more manageable parts; to listen to others and absorb what they say; to soak up information indiscriminately - like a sponge, and sort through it later; to focus your mind on purposeful study and observation; and to aim for your goals, not just talk about them. If you take the Twins' childlike wonder and innate everyday wisdom under your broad wings, they can help you to soar higher than you ever dreamed possible. Only then, when fuelled by this opposing brand of power, will you find your life gaining, literally, upward momentum.

MAGIC, DRAWING, ATTRACTION, SPELLS, RITUALS, WISHING & POWER

A Note on the Universe

Within each of us resides the merging of the Sun and the Moon, the dance of the constellations, the vibrations of the planets, and the vast microcosm and macrocosm of the entire *Universe*. Uni means 'one' and Verse means 'song'; therefore, the word Universe literally means 'One Song'. If you learn to tune yourself in, you can even hear it!

What is Magic?

Magic is a kind of special energy that is beyond description, and like most kinds of energy it has its own rules and ways of being manipulated. It remains an elusive term, and no definition has ever really found Universal acceptance. Attempts to separate it from superstition, religion and other-worldly phenomena on the one hand, and 'science' on the other, are ridden with difficulties. However slippery the term 'magic' might be, there is a general agreement that most of us wish for more of its presence in our lives and often fall short of achieving this wish.

Those performing spells, 'asking the Universe', wishing, praying, or undertaking rituals, are using this very special energy to draw things to them. Learning to manipulate energy in these ways is never hard (and shouldn't be), but it can be complex and does require knowledge, practice, creativity, patience and above all, imagination. Most of us use simple magic every day, whether by saying little prayers, making wishes, visualising, and exchanging - sending out and receiving - good, positive or hopeful vibes. When you understand that all the forces and magic you need are *within* you, and you learn to *believe* in that power, you are then able to make all manner of changes to your life and, most importantly, yourself.

Magic is an invisible force which connects and permeates everything. Every thought you have and every action you take, will affect the strength of this force, and can be influenced and directed towards a specific purpose by using certain means. The most important of these are your intentions, facing in the direction of your desired outcome, your will and your *belief* that it works. The more you want something to happen, and the clearer you can visualise the desired outcome, the stronger your will and feelings towards it will be, ensuring an avalanche of amazing people, events and circumstances will flow into your experiences, gathering speed, momentum and power as it nears your goal or dream.

The Universe (or whichever higher power you believe in) works for us and through us. Ideas are given to us but they must be carried out *through* us, in the form of asking or acting or performing a ritual or casting a specific spell. The Universe's abundance is your abundance, and it flows through your mind into manifestation. The Universe or Divine Being in which you believe, gives you the necessary ideas and clothes them with all that is needed to bring them into form when we ask *believing*.

Based on ancient human beliefs, systems and superstitions, declaring what you want and acting out your deepest desires can actually help to make things happen. Magical ideas include the notion that thought affects matter and that the trained imagination can alter the physical world, that all aspects of the Universe are interdependent and that we can discover connections and correspondences between everyday occurrences and cosmic, or Divine, energies. A miracle or a wish coming true can suggest something is going on that extends beyond the laws of nature, that something unseen has occurred; but just because we cannot see it or touch it, it doesn't mean it's not there. Magic exists, especially if you truly believe it does, but science is so far incapable of capturing its essence or the rationale behind it. Personally, I prefer to leave that task to the higher powers of the Universe.

To help your dreams come true and to use your inborn power to its full effect, you can employ boosters based on the special energies and qualities of your Sun sign. These 'boosters' are chosen to be in alignment with the purpose of a particular goal, and contain energies of their own which will enhance the strength of your spell, prayer, ritual or 'asking'. Specific magical energies can be invoked by carrying out a spell or ceremony using specific herbs or colours, or on a particular day of the week, according to either your Sun sign (to heighten the power of the asking), and/or that is in sympathy with that for which you are asking (I have included days of the week for other Sun signs and spell types).

Some materials and boosters you can use to increase the power, magic or energy in any area of your life include: candles, wish lists (written on an appropriate piece of paper written with a specially-chosen writing tool), symbols, affirmations, chants, incense, herbs and flowers, locations, colours, days of the week, elements, crystals and gemstones, animal symbols, charms, talismans, amulets, gods and goddesses, essential oils, planetary hours and your Solar totem animals. All are covered, some more briefly than others, for your very special Sun sign to radiate the energy to powerfully draw your wildest dreams towards you!

Overall, it pays to remember that the Universe (or whatever higher power/s or force/s you happen to believe in) creates *through* you that to which you give your attention. What you contemplate becomes the law of your being, and through your pure unwavering belief, is eventually brought through to manifestation on the material plane. What you think about is entirely up to you. But just be mindful that whatever you think about the most becomes your dominant thought, then your main point of attraction, and is ultimately magnified until it becomes your reality or your experience. So choose your thoughts with care. And to quote Ralph Waldo Emerson, "Be careful what you set your heart upon, for it will surely be yours." I carry a copy of this beautiful prophecy in my purse as its words resonate so strongly with me. In other words, be mindful about what you're wishing for, for you will most probably get it, whether it's good or bad - magic, after all, doesn't discriminate. Just make your dominant thoughts good ones, and you will attract everything you set your heart and intentions upon. Good luck!

ASTROLOGY & MAGIC

"Everyone practices magic, whether they realise it or not, for magic is the art of attracting particular influences, events and situations within human life. Magic is a natural phenomenon because the Universe is reflexive, responding to human thoughts, aspirations and desires ..."
David Fideler, *Jesus Christ, Sun of God*

Astrology is the most sublime of the occult * sciences, while at the same time it is one of the most practical for everyday application, for it divines the human soul itself. The cosmos, particularly the patterns that formed across it at the exact moment we were born, indicates the road along which our mental and spiritual endowments are likely to impel us, therefore enabling us to prepare in advance for life's battles, pitfalls, milestones, celebrations and of course to make the utmost of opportunities. Such is the magic of the human mind, that it can 'see' into the future and relive the past without having to be physically present in either, and when combined with astrological *knowing*, particularly the knowing that springs from understanding some of the dynamics of our natal chart, however basic, our inner - and outer - magic can be lifted to phenomenal heights.

In ancient times, not only was astrology the ardent study of the most learned and powerful minds, but among the masses of ordinary people its authority and guidance was accepted and followed without question. How this powerful knowledge was used was - and still is - up to the individual, but all who used it applied it to their perceived advantage.

As primitive humans observed the skies, no doubt they gradually realised that certain stars upon which their fate depended accompanied the seasons, or certain times of the year. They may also have reasoned that if governed their fate, they also governed their bodies, and it is therefore conceivable that the skies were associated with Divine influence. Certain celestial influences were believed to emanate from the thirty-six decans of the signs, and the mysterious but apparent effect that they exercised upon humans were thought to be due to a subtle ether shed by the heavenly stars and spheres on the Earth, that affected not only people, but also other animals, plants and minerals. For the ancient mind, linking magic with astrology may have also provided a much needed sense of predictability and patterns.

Early astrologers named and made associations with the imaginary divisions of the twelve signs and the twelve houses, and people born under a certain sign were said to inherit to an extent, its properties and nature. They also believed that the influence of the planets and stars corresponded with the medicinal properties of certain plants and minerals. They therefore asserted that the influence of a star or planetary position would affect the type of medicine or healing they would offer a subject to attain the most beneficial outcome. Throughout the writings of early philosophers and theorists, there is constant reference to this unmistakable mystic connection between the seven known planets and Earthly affairs and ailments. The seven metals were connected with the seven planets, to which the seven colours and the seven transformations were added. So the alchemist came to share the astrological doctrine that each planet ruled some mineral: The Sun ruled gold, the Moon silver, Mars iron, Venus copper, Saturn lead, Jupiter tin, and Mercury quicksilver. Consequently, in alchemical symbolism the same sign came to represent the metal and its corresponding planet.

In subsequent years, astrology became closely related to alchemical knowledge and development, and the alchemist came to be regarded as an authority not only on the transmutation of metals, but also on astrology and magic. This goes some of the way to explaining how magic and divination, which had always been inseparably bound up with astrology, came to be associated with alchemy. In all the occult sciences, the supreme power was believed to be in the stars above, and from their mysterious emanations all the metals, crystals, minerals, plants and herbs derived their special properties over time. Further, as alchemy became ever more spiritual and concerned with more abstract and philosophical concepts, eventually it was considered that the transmutation of lead into gold was simply a metaphor for the transformation of base matter, in this case the human soul, into a much purer and higher state of wisdom and being.

The Sun and Moon were believed to have greater influence over the human body than all the other heavenly bodies, and to exert their influence in various ways whenever they entered a certain sign of the zodiac. And although the Moon was traditionally regarded as the most important factor of a horoscope, the Sun has come into its own in later centuries, with the result that almost everyone knows their Sun sign but only those who have delved deeper are aware of the sign their natal Moon falls in. For this reason, I have chosen to focus this book series on the twelve Sun signs, as this is what the majority of people are most familiar with.

The following pages contain methods, energies, materials and objects which may be used to increase the magic and power of your Sun sign's influence upon you. Precious stones, flowers, colours and so on, are regarded as having a potent effect upon good fortune by attuning your mind to receive harmonious vibrations from the astral forces that surround you.

Finally, a basic working knowledge of basic astronomy and astrology is an asset when working with luck, abundance, wealth and personal power. You can attract more of these things when you align yourself with the workings of the wider Universe, the movement of the Sun, stars, Moon and planets and become aware of the correlations between the outer cycles of the skies and the inner cycles within yourself. Also, for those who are knowledgeable about Moon phases, equinoxes and solstices, a world of lucky possibilities can also magically open up to you. You don't need to know about astrology's deepest complexities to understand how everything interrelates; just learning the basics will give you an edge - and hopefully the following lucky tips will provide you with at least a small glimpse into the insights gleaned from your Sun sign, which I am certain will endow upon you the potential for amazing results to manifest in your life - and maybe even a step up one further rung towards the heavens!

* The word 'occult' comes from the Latin *occultus*, which literally means 'knowledge of the hidden'.

USING COLOURS, CRYSTALS, DEITIES, PLANTS, FOODS & MATERIAL SUBSTANCES FOR INCREASING POWER & MAGNETISING MAGIC

Alchemist, reformer and mystic Henry Cornelius Agrippa, born in 1486, in his principal work, *On Occult Philosophy*, expressed his belief in the doctrines of astrology and in the theory that the spirit of the world exists in the body of the world, just as the human spirit exists in the body of man. He contended that this spirit also abounds in the celestial bodies and descends in the rays of stars, so that the things influenced by their rays become conformable to them. By this spirit every occult property is conveyed into metals, stones, herbs and animals, through the Sun, Moon and planets, and even through the stars beyond and higher than the planets. A firm believer in the efficacy of charms, he stated that they may "be worn on the body bound to any part of it or hung around the neck, changing sickness into health or health into sickness." I believe the same effect could be applied to wishing and the thinking of positive thoughts, to mean, "Changing thoughts and dreams into manifest reality." He also recommended that these charms be worn in the form of finger rings (that have been created using the materials in agreement and harmony with your Sun Sign's magical energy).

Material substances are connected with abstract purposes by a complex but highly usable and accessible system of correspondences. Use these time-honoured connections in your own spells and wishes to magnetise your desires to you. The following pages will give you some materials, energies, forces and ideas you can summon the power of in order to enhance your magic and luck.

PLANETS

The Planetary influence of the day is important when 'asking' for something. If you are wishing for luck, for example, try working with your Sun sign's inherent energies combined with the perfect day of the week for it. So a Sagittarian might try using his natural intellect and articulate expression, to ask for love and romance on a Friday, which is Venus's Day and Venus is renowned for being a romantic planet, or better still, ask for love on a Thursday, which is Jupiter's Day, planetary ruler of Sagittarius, at the time of day when Venus's influence is at its most powerful (information about planetary hours for each day of the week can be found on the Internet or in books on the subject, and can be complex and detailed. It is an art to memorise the correct times, days and energies for the correct spells. If you are determined enough to achieve your dream or goal however, you will be determined enough to put in the research to do it properly!) Here is a very simplified list of the days of the week and their meanings:

DAYS OF THE WEEK & THEIR POWERS

MONDAY ★ Moon
Cancer

The Divine feminine, changes, intuition, emotions, secrets, dealing with women, purity, goodness, perfection, unity, psychic ability, magic, spirituality, invoking a goddess's or angel's guidance, anything that fluctuates, contracts, increases or decreases.

TUESDAY ★ Mars
Aries & Scorpio

Enthusiasm, competition, passion, energy, courage, protection, victory, anything requiring assertiveness, standing up for yourself, or a 'fighting spirit', determination, vitality, sexuality, self-confidence, men's power, men's mysteries, drive, ambition, achievement, triumph, masculinity.

WEDNESDAY ★ Mercury
Gemini & Virgo

Education, travel, exams, study, communication, making connections, thinking, dealing with siblings, writing and speaking, knowledge, learning, adaptability, charm, youth, absorbing information.

THURSDAY ★ Jupiter
Sagittarius & Pisces

Increase and expansion of anything (remember to be careful what you wish for), luck, growth, influence, worldly power, accomplishment, fulfilment, gambling, philosophy, higher education, abundance, optimism.

FRIDAY ★ Venus
Taurus & Libra

Love, luxury, the arts, indulgence, beauty, marriage, money, prosperity, fertility, women's power, women's mysteries, grace, charm, appeal, hope, pleasure, decorating, self-worth, self-esteem, personal values, business partnerships, romance, creativity, sharing, bonding.

SATURDAY ★ Saturn
Capricorn & Aquarius

Long-term goals, career, institutions, establishments, security, investments, karma, reversal, structure, protection, solitude, privacy, determination, ending, blocking, renewing, transforming, anything to do with the public.

SUNDAY ★ Sun
Leo

All-purpose, success, wishes, generosity, happiness, optimism, spirit/essence, recognition, health, vitality, material wealth, invoking a god's aid or guidance, personal empowerment, spirituality, the Divine masculine.

YOUR NATAL MOON PHASE

Although this book is aimed at enhancing your life through the energy of your Sun sign, a bit of Lunar help can give your wishing a boost! As well as using the planetary days and hours system to add a bit of zest to your wish fulfilment, try combining your Sun sign's power periods with your natal Moon phase (your natal Moon phase can be calculated using a number of sources on the internet, or through an astrologer), or even studying which constellation the Moon is situated in at certain times, to increase the power of your spells and asking rituals. For example, you might like to 'ask' for a promotion at work during a New/Waxing Moon period, particularly if the Moon happens to fall under an auspicious sign for career advancement, such as Capricorn. Your natal Moon phase can also be used to similar effect, by researching when your Moon phase will coincide with a certain Lunar constellation position.

In most astrological interpretations the Sun is regarded as the most important, central feature of a natal chart. But to many the Moon is equally, if not more, important than the Sun sign. Many ancient cultures considered the Moon sign to be more significant. The Moon passes through the 12 signs about every 2.5 days, usually covering the whole zodiac in around 27.3 days. The Moon symbolises our inner world, the world of feeling, emotions, habitual responses, instincts, intuition, security and the subconscious. It describes our nurturing style and needs, our emotional response to life, our attitudes and likely reactions to others, our instinctive and habitual responses, the receptive feminine side of ourselves, our experience of our mother or mother figure, and our childhood experience. It represents the soul. In relationships it symbolises how we like to be nurtured and cared for, and the potential depth of our involvement on personal intimate levels.

For many centuries, people across the world have recognised that the Moon influences the affairs of all living things on planet Earth. The waxing Moon appears to have a drawing, increasing and enhancing effect, whereas the waning Moon has a decreasing, receding and withdrawing effect. All things that come into being are stamped with the qualities of the prevailing Moon stage. It seems that people born during certain Lunar phases tend to share specific attributes with other people born during this same phase. In turn, their attributes will be subtly different from those of individuals born during any of the other stages in the Moon cycle. Knowing exactly which phase of the Moon you were born under gives you all kinds of extraordinarily valuable insights into your character, emotions, behaviour and motivations in life. It can make you aware of your deepest underlying drives, the fundamental purpose that you are drawn towards in life and the contribution you can make to others and society during the course of your lifetime. This knowledge may enable you to intuit and make the most of your own personal cyclical pattern that you go through each month, and allow you to know when the most auspicious periods of time are for you and your affairs, nurture yourself and channel your energies in the most positive directions.

Because this Lunar pattern repeats itself every month, you will find that you can even pace yourself on a long-term basis. This will enable you to effectively target your efforts and goals on periods of time that you know will be potentially fortunate for you. You may in fact find that your birth phase corresponds with the days of the month when you have abundant energy, feel inspired and can generate new ideas with ease. During this period, you should work towards the fruition of your efforts, bring your dreams into light and reach for the stars!

The Lunar Phases Are:

★ New Moon
★ First/Waxing Crescent
★ First Quarter
★ Waxing Gibbous Moon
★ Full Moon
★ Waning Gibbous / Disseminating Moon
★ Last Quarter
★ Waning Crescent / Balsamic Moon
★ Back to the New Moon

the next Full Moon. Magical workings for gain, increase or bringing things to you should be initiated when the Moon is waxing (or New, going from Dark to Full). A time for divination of all kinds, spells of spiritual intention, and for any creative project you wish to see birthed, with magical and fruitful results.

While making a wish within the first forty-eight hours after the New Moon is a powerful way of helping it come to fruition, the most potent time for making wishes is actually within the first eight hours of the exact time of its position. Write down your wish list within this first eight hours on a piece of appropriately coloured paper with a special writing tool, and be sure to capture the essence of your wish by wording it in a way that charges your emotions and simply feels 'right'. Make a maximum of ten wishes (less is perfectly fine too), as making too many wishes might disperse their energy too much to be effective. After writing down your list and releasing your wishes to the Universe in whichever form you feel happy with, keep your list and check on it in a few days', weeks' or months' time to assess whether anything has shifted in the direction of your listed dreams, desires or goals. I'll bet it has - or at the very least, something even better has arrived in its place!

Although the first forty-eight hours after the New Moon is the most potent time to make a special wish, you can begin Waxing Moon magic when you can see the crescent in the sky and continue until the day before the Full Moon. The closer to the Full Moon, the more intense the energies. In fact, a personally devised ritual using any special Lunar-associated materials over three days up to and including the Full Moon is excellent for something you require urgently or within a short timeframe.

In some cultures, people turn over silver coins or jewellery three times when the crescent Moon appears in the sky and make a wish. As the Moon grows, it is believed that prosperity and good fortune will grow too.

While the New Moon is not known as a time for 'banishing' or releasing things we no longer want in our lives, I feel that if we are to ask and wish for things, we need to make room to receive them. Making room means that the Universe can slot it right into our lives where we have cleared our paths for it. Clutter, unwanted things, unhappy relationships, possessions that no longer serve us, are all things we can banish. So, to help what you are asking for come into your life quicker, the New Moon is a particularly opportune time to throw a few things out so you can make way for the new and clear up some space for that which you are wishing for. What are you waiting for? Start creating a space for your wishes today!

FULL MOON

In astronomical terms, the Full Moon occurs 14 days after the New Moon, on the day when the Moon sets at the same time the Sun rises, or conversely. The two luminaries are effectively facing each other, with the Earth in between, the Sun shining its light onto the reflective Moon, giving it the fully lit up appearance of a giant, bright, perfectly round sphere. Indeed, its entire face is bathed in sunlight. A Lunar eclipse can only occur at the Full Moon, when the Sun, Moon and Earth are all in line, and the Earth hides the lit side of the Moon to us.

In astrological terms, a Full Moon occurs at the time when the Sun and Moon are 180 degrees apart inside the zodiac, and therefore positioned in opposite signs, forming an opposition aspect.

The highest energy occurs at the Full Moon, making this is a powerful time for all manner of magical workings. Use the Full Moon phase for any immediate need, a sudden boost of power or courage, psychic protection, a change of career or location, travel, healing acute health conditions, the consummation of love or a commitment, justice, ambition and promotion of all kinds. This phase lasts approximately 3 days - 24 hours before the exact Full Moon, the day of, and 24 hours after it, according to many sources - giving us 3 full days to perform our spells. However, we are not strictly limited to a three-day period; the power of this phase can actually be accessed for seven days - three days prior to, the night of, and the three days after the Full Moon. The Full Moon period is when the Moon is at her most powerful, being the most luminous and radiant part of the cycle. Known as the 'high tide' of psychic power, the Full Moon represents culmination, climax, fulfilment and abundance. The Full Moon governs all kinds of magic, including manifestation, banishing, and is particularly good for calling forth protection and heightening your intuitive abilities. The Full Moon contains magic that calls forth personal power, fertility, spiritual development, and psychic awareness. Cleansing of ritual tools, crystals, wish lists, Tarot decks, and the like can be done during this phase. Magic worked during the Full Moon often takes one complete cycle to come to fruition. Try also reaffirming your desires during the New Moon to give them an added nudge in the right direction.

LAST QUARTER OR WANING MOON

In astronomical terms, the Last Quarter, or Waning Moon, occurs twenty-one days after the New Moon. The time difference between the rising and setting of the two luminaries is reduced to what it was at the First Quarter. Viewed from the Earth, the Moon resembles a crescent whose lit up area is decreasing in size, forming the shape of a capital C.

In astrological terms, the Waning Moon occurs when the Sun and Moon are positioned at ninety degree angles of each other in the zodiac, forming the square aspect again. However, during this phase, the Sun is instead *ahead* of the Moon.

The Waning Moon represents the Lunar cycle from Full to Dark. Any spells and magic performed during this period is based purely around banishing and releasing. It could involve releasing things which no longer serve you (such as behaviours, material things, relationships and attitudes), banishing negative energies, and removing obstacles which are standing in the way of achieving your goals or dreams. The Waning Moon is the best time for cleansing, gently releasing, eliminating, expelling and completion. It is of great assistance when you are wanting to let go of something, or someone, gradually. The Dark of the Moon, the period when the Moon is no longer visible to the naked eye, until the New Moon, is the most useful time for divination of all kinds.

★ What is your natal Moon phase type? Can you think of ways you can combine it with the power of your Sun sign to effect change and bring about wonderful happenings? ★

HARNESSING YOUR PERSONAL MOON MAGIC ★ MOON IN SAGITTARIUS

When the Moon is in your sign of Sagittarius, it is a great time for working magic around: Adventure, long-distance travel plans, expansion of anything, generosity, mercy, faith, optimism, charity and hope. Suggested operations could be around rituals and spells to expand any project, vision or talent, and to find understanding and meaning in challenging situations. Invoke the Lunar Sagittarius for breadth of vision, honesty, open-mindedness, and all creative and expansive ventures. It is also an opportune time to broaden your horizons, strengthen your personal faith, and cultivate awareness of others, as well as generosity and giving. With the Moon in Sagittarius, you can also seek to learn and study spiritual practices and religions. If you wish for your cup to runneth over with anything (love, zest, money, friendship, travel), a Sagittarius Moon is the time to ask for it, for his is the energy which will expand the horizons of possibility in your life.

THE MOON ★ WHAT IT REPRESENTS IN THE HUMAN PSYCHE & NATAL CHART

The Moon in the sky shines with the reflected light of the Sun. Although not a planet, the Moon is our nearest celestial neighbour and exerts a great influence upon us. The gravitational pull of the Moon affects our body fluids, which contribute to about 90 per cent of our biological make-up. It moves at approximately half a degree per hour and takes an average of 27.3 days to pass through all twelve zodiac signs, staying in each for around 2.5 days.

In astrology the Moon corresponds with the way in which we reflect and respond to what is going on around us. It has to do with our feelings, emotions and instincts and, in the same way the Moon influences the tides on planet Earth, it symbolises the ebb and flow of our emotional nature, our moods, fluctuations and changeability. The Moon is the archetype of the Mother, which is within us all, and represents the primary feminine principle in the natal chart. It is through the Moon that we express our parental instincts - caring, nurturing, protecting, sensitivity. The Moon has links with the past and the subconscious and it is from this almost primitive source that our natural instinctual forces flow.

The Moon is essentially a feminine principle and associates with the inner personality, receptivity, passivity and inward-oriented feelings. It can act as an inner guide to the deeper self, the unconscious self, figures half-shrouded in mystery, linking the hidden personal world of the subconscious to the clearer world of personal awareness.

The Moon is the innermost core of our being, private feelings, habitual reactions and subconscious habits. It is the caring, nurturing sustainer of life, the 'mother' of the zodiac. It tells us about how we seek security, our urge to nurture, our nurturing style, our responses and feelings and moods. The innermost core of our being, private feelings, subconscious habits. It is concerned with habits, mothering, habitual/instinctive responses and personality. It is our karma, our soul, our past.

The Moon represents our mother or mother figure, our feminine side, maternal instinct, our nurturing style and needs, our unconscious self, our emotional reactions, the subconscious, our feelings, instincts, intuition, receptivity, habits, what we need to feel secure, fluctuations, cycles, moods, and our childhood. Its position in the birth chart is very significant, because as well as revealing feminine qualities and the potential gentleness and tenderness of a being, the Moon also reveals important information about the experiences and expression of the five senses.

The Moon is essentially receptive and passive; it reflects the life experience rather than initiating it. Fluctuating and cyclical, the Moon is the planet (although technically a satellite) of the childhood experience, and instinctual reactions. It represents the mother (a child's experience and expectations of their mother), maternal instincts and the feminine principle, indicating how strongly these manifest in an individual, male or female.

As it represents what our childhood experience is likely to be, and childhood is essentially a time where our consciousness has not yet fully developed, our Moon sign traits seem to be more apparent in our younger years. We will usually show our Moon sign traits more so than our Sun sign traits during this developing period of infancy and early childhood, until we have the presence of mind to more consciously develop our ego and true core self (the Sun).

The symbol for the Moon ☽ is a representation of its crescent in its waxing phase from new to full, but it can also be seen as two half circles - these form a bowl shape, a receptacle, a feminine container that 'receives' and 'holds' anything put into it. The half circle, unlike the full circle of the Sun, is finite and incomplete, almost as if striving for wholeness.

The Moon represents our *soul*.

YOUR MOON SIGN

The Sun / Moon Polarity
Conscious & Unconscious, Night & Day, Yin & Yang

"Man does, woman is."
Edward Edinger

Your Moon Sign, representing your soul, and your Sun sign, representing your spirit, work together to form the foundation of your basic personality, expression and nature. If you know what your Moon sign is, look it up below and read how it works with your Sagittarian Sun to blend your mind, soul and spirit.

♈ **With the Moon in ARIES, Sun in Sagittarius,** you are likely to be ★ Heroic, passionate, outspoken, pioneering, original, arrogant, extroverted, optimistic, egocentric, showy, forthright, a big talker, expressive, fearless, self-assured, courageous, bold, restless, impatient, on the go, adventurous, direct, active, blunt but sincere, emotionally naïve, self-interested, impulsive, impractical, progressive, alert, childish, impetuous, enthusiastic, independent, genuine, innocently charming, hopeful, emotionally demanding, warm, generous, exaggerating, competitive, expansive, sociable, infectiously enthusiastic, unsubtle, honest, explorative, assertive, confident, insensitive, buoyant, energetic, driven to succeed, bossy, popular, domineering, emotionally reckless, forward-looking, lively, witty, frank, bright, an individualist, and possess a touchy ego and moral integrity, as well as being a maverick with a crusading temperament.

Sun/Moon Harmony Rating ★ *7.5 out of 10* **

♉ **With the Moon in TAURUS, Sun in Sagittarius,** you are likely to be ★ Conflicted between freedom and foundation, driven, a down-to-Earth dreamer, restrainedly idealistic, argumentative, materialistic, extravagant, luxury-loving, expansive, pleasure-seeking, a connoisseur, easy going, romantic, a modestly passionate learner, big-hearted, appreciative, seductive, seeking of the good life, calm but expansive, approachable, affable, a slave to your expensive tastes, in possession of entrenched beliefs, unshakable, measuredly optimistic, sensitive to beauty and philosophy, artistic, creative, sexy, sensual, steadily aspiring, tenacious, physically and mentally robust, devoted yet flighty, restless yet grounded, gently charming, faithful, bossy, friendly, warm-hearted, generous, productive, a practical philosopher, enthusiastic about making money, an entrepreneur, ambitious, strong-willed, philanthropic, in possession of a strong sense of self, and dedicated to activating your inspired ideas in the real, material world.

Sun/Moon Harmony Rating ★ *6.5 out of 10*

♊ **With the Moon in GEMINI, Sun in Sagittarius,** you are likely to be ★ Persuasive, charming, sociable, witty, inquisitive, blunt, mentally dextrous, emotionally agile, flexible, deft, cheeky, a free spirit, changeable, non-committal, philosophical yet superficial, friendly, bright, breezy, versatile, adaptable, quick, careless, stimulating, flippant, vital, perceptive, clever, inspiring, curious, childlike, full of wonder and awe, emotionally impulsive, vivacious, zany, inconsistent, expressive, restless, easily bored, active, inspired, a live wire, unsubtle, direct, humorous, funny, communicative, socially aware, unsentimental, naïve, immature, irresponsible, intellectually capable, unreliable, zestful, an opportunist, cunning, funny, easily swept away by ideas and concepts, open towards and perceptive of new ideas, idealistic, intellectual, fun-loving, squandering of your natural talents, too busy to deal with feelings, scattered, with too many irons in the fire, and in possession of the gift of the gab and a sunny, breezy and light-hearted disposition.

Sun/Moon Harmony Rating ★ *8 out of 10*

♋ **With the Moon in CANCER, Sun in Sagittarius,** you are likely to be ★ Sensitive, affable, temperamental, friendly but private, uplifting, an enthusiastic supporter of others, clannish, devoted, romantic, a prophetic visionary, over-extended, understatedly brilliant, in possession of pizzazz and a sense of theatrics, charming, affectionate, sensual, demonstrative, inspired to help others, changeable, inconsistent, moody, adaptable, torn between security and freedom, deeply feeling, emotionally charged, richly imaginative, genuinely caring, boundlessly hopeful, indirectly self-assertive, intuitive, idealistic, emotionally expressive, dramatic, passionate about family, subtly persuasive, tuned into others, insightful, helpful, giving, compassionate, kind-hearted, generous, creative, kind, gentle-spirited, helpful, companionable, a sensitive individualist, emotionally nurturing, defensive, ruled equally by your mind *and* your heart, and occasionally moved to dramatic outbursts which may undermine your greatest talents and achievements.

Sun/Moon Harmony Rating ★ 8 out of 10

♌ **With the Moon in LEO, Sun in Sagittarius**, you are likely to be ★ Pompous, radiant, vain, noble, a gambler, involved, overbearing, pure-of-heart, inflated, gregarious, flamboyant, egotistical, proud, independent, warm-hearted, individualistic, chivalrous, autocratic, impatient, sociable, playful, dramatic, fearless, bold, artistic, generous to a fault, extravagant, charismatic, in love with love, passionate, an effective leader, zestful, vital, uplifting, immediate, sulky, childish, demanding, bossy, enthusiastic, active, adventurous, friendly, a good leader, enthusiastically romantic, explorative, open, powerful, extroverted, self-interested, honest, inclined to get carried away by drama and fun, idealistic, direct, controlling, expressive, ambitious, grandiose, theatrical, emotionally warm, luxury-loving, demonstrative, expressive, stylish, creatively imaginative, optimistic, larger than life, honourable, and able to inspire and uplift others with your vitality and radiance.

Sun/Moon Harmony Rating ★ *7.5 out of 10* **

♍ **With the Moon in VIRGO, Sun in Sagittarius,** you are likely to be ★ A curious mixture of devotion to obligations and to freedom, intelligent, reasonable, just, hot and cold, rapport-seeking, restless yet dutiful, socially concerned, judgemental, bold but cautious, clever, sharp-witted, logical, intellectually precise and discerning, able to convey ideas easily, objective, discriminating, genuine, an intellectual perfectionist, snobby, cavalier yet careful, able to categorise knowledge, quietly charming, uncomfortable with emotions, pedantic, boldly dogmatic, morally sound, humorously tactful, academic, nervous, highly strung, striving, a pragmatic philosophiser, studious, an avid learner, outspoken yet reserved, bossy yet diffident, helpful, generous, serious, academic, kind-hearted, genuinely caring, mentally alert, efficient, mentally dextrous, straightforward, adaptable, quietly passionate, motivated, intolerant of others' weaknesses, analytical, critical, altruistic, conscientious, effective, self-disciplined, bright, devoted to ideals, dry-witted, zestful yet uptight, and able to dedicate all your efforts into something worthwhile.

Sun/Moon Harmony Rating ★ *6 out of 10*

♎ **With the Moon in LIBRA, Sun in Sagittarius,** you are likely to be ★ Stylish, charming, sociable, refined, easy going, likeable, clever, effervescent, lively, classy, extravagant, intellectually precocious, gregarious, able to see life from endlessly new vantage points, affectionate, confident but indecisive, convivial, amorous, gracious, warmly sincere, positive, observant, socially aware, popular, approachable, ethereal and spirited, courteous, eager for life, tolerant, ingenious, chivalrous, accessible, civilised, hospitable, hedonistic, interested in others, romantically idealistic, endearing, loving of people, colourfully persuasive, procrastinating, outgoing, a generous spirit, prophetic, artistic, creative, gracefully enthusiastic, flirtatious, inspiring, hopeful, vain, entertaining, emotionally naïve, a philosopher, a maverick but a seeker of justice, and conflicted between independence and needing others.

Sun/Moon Harmony Rating ★ *8.5 out of 10*

♏ **With the Moon in SCORPIO, Sun in Sagittarius,** you are likely to be ★ Confident, intense, sociable, judicial and exacting, vivid, feisty, satirical, keenly instinctive, keen to acquire self-knowledge, volatile, magnetic, highly motivated, self-dramatising, socially powerful, forceful, blunt, intelligent, scrutinising, questioning, ambitious, highly charged, extreme, active, aggressively optimistic, over-zealous, undeterred, morally intense, pushy, keenly insightful, philosophical, investigative, narcissistic, fanatical, self-destructive, a troublemaker when bored, insatiable, strong-willed, dominating, passionate, unyielding, purposeful, sharp, over-indulgent, highly sexed, seductive, overbearing, extremely resilient, persuasive, charismatic, devoted to truth at any cost, fiercely independent, penetrative, emotionally expressive, courageously dedicated, compulsive, perceptive, self-reliant, exacting, manipulative, possess an unshakeable belief in yourself and others' individual worth, and in possession of a strong sense of self and personal integrity.

Sun/Moon Harmony Rating ★ *7 out of 10*

♐ **With the Moon in SAGITTARIUS, Sun in Sagittarius,** you are likely to be ★ Big-hearted, warm, all-embracing, entertaining, wise-cracking, restless, a perennial student of life, noble, a wanderer, frank, tolerant, talkative, eager, impatient, gregarious, feisty, broad-minded, fiercely independent, sincere, dazzling, outdoorsy, idealistic, explorative, an avid traveller, honest, adventurous, impatient with petty details and restrictions, principled, moralistic, full of faith, benevolent, adverse to limitations, sloppy, irresponsible, a visionary, self-confident, outspoken, prone to preach, loving of a challenge, far-sighted, insensitive, blunt, a daredevil, rash, inquisitive, self-assured, zestful, emotionally reckless, a free spirit, in possession of a keen sense of humour, extravagant, careless, contagiously optimistic, inspiring, outrageous, aspiring, trusting, naïve, expansive, verbose, philosophical, freedom-seeking, and have an intense moral certainty, residing in the realm of limitless possibilities and being guided by reason rather than emotion.

Sun/Moon Harmony Rating ★ *7 out of 10*

♑ **With the Moon in CAPRICORN, Sun in Sagittarius,** you are likely to be ★ Facile yet profound, verbose, independent, steadfast, broad-minded, ambitious, dogmatically blunt, opportunistic, power-grabbing, driven, reasonable, moralistic, rational, logical, articulated, detached, realistic, pragmatically philosophical, a practical dreamer, tough-minded, forceful, aggressive, assertive, assertive, delightfully witty, sensual, ardent, enterprising, astute, blunt, overpowering, committed to worthy causes, driven to succeed, unstoppable, unemotional, ruled by reason and logic, charged, intense, dressed for success, profoundly wise, efficient, personally honourable, bold, fearless, socially uptight, sardonically humorous, and in possession of an overall attitude of 'shoot for the stars' - while remaining firmly planted in the Earth at the same time.

Sun/Moon Harmony Rating ★ *7.5 out of 10*

♒ **With the Moon in AQUARIUS, Sun in Sagittarius,** you are likely to be ★ Sharp-witted, a nutty professor, a mad scientist, mentally agile, independent, freedom-seeking, philanthropic, eccentric, a broad-minded humanitarian, intellectual, restless, a people person, globally socially aware, incisive, unrealistic, gregarious, a high-minded genius, full of bright ideas, congenial, sociable, friendly, tolerant, extroverted, academic, shocking, highly idealistic, emotionally detached, unconventional, a revolutionary, loquacious, a social activist, unpredictable, evasive, paradoxical, unconventional, honest, original, forward-moving, inventive, impersonal in relationships, clear-headed, charismatic, a social visionary, a truth-seeker, impatient with practical details, irresponsible, absent-minded, highly observant, acutely aware of the human condition, progressive, scientifically oriented, prophetic, objective, living an unusual lifestyle in some way, out of touch, abstract, open to the unusual, emotionally naïve, blunt and insensitive when comparing people with your ideals, freedom-loving, unorthodox, idealistic, impractical, loyal, exceptionally individual, socially conscious, committed to your ideals, a law unto yourself, in possession of an eternal sense of hope and belief in others, and interested in making friends right across the fascinating broad spectrum of human viewpoints.

Sun/Moon Harmony Rating ★ *9 out of 10*

♓ **With the Moon in PISCES, Sun in Sagittarius,** you are likely to be ★ Deeply idealistic, creative, unassuming, imaginative, easily swept away, giving, warm, intuitive, romantic, emotionally expressive, prophetic, insightful, perceptive, enthusiastically mystical, enriching to others, wistful, lacking in focus and discrimination, trusting, naïve, a chaser of spiritual rainbows, philosophical, elusive, receptive, sociable yet withdrawn, procrastinating, good-natured, hearty, intriguing, friendly, emotional, full of faith, fervent, sentimental, far-sighted but dreamy, impulsive, careless, tolerant, accepting, irresponsible, understanding, independent but vulnerable, a keen poet, altruistic, a visionary, generous, receptive, artistic, reverent, empathetic, impressionable, innocent, easily swayed, gullible, impractical, evasive, emotionally intelligent, adaptable, adverse to limitations and boundaries, dramatic, hopeful, able to mix and work with all types of people, aware of the needs of others, and in possession of a refreshing philosophy of life.

Sun/Moon Harmony Rating ★ *9 out of 10*

** If your Moon is in Aries or Leo, your Sun and Moon will form what is known in astrology as a trine aspect. This aspect is the easiest, most flowing and harmonious astrological aspect, ensuring that your Sun and Moon, or spirit and soul, are well integrated. With both luminaries in Fire signs, this gives them the best possible degree of complementary energy - a blending of the elements suggests a balanced expression of personality. One drawback of the trine aspect lies in the fact that its easy flow can be *too* harmonious; if our path is too smooth and difficulties don't arise to challenge us from time to time, we can often become lazy and complacent, stunting our growth and spiritual evolution. As Fire signs, you share the art of vitality, zest, enthusiasm, broad-mindedness, affability, idealism, independence, drive, ambition, force, affection, warm-heartedness, generosity, sociability, and have extravagant tastes, but may be temperamental, dramatic, overbearing, egocentric, restless, bossy, insensitive, careless, arrogant and self-centred.

YOUR BODY & HEALTH

"A physician without a knowledge of astrology has no right to call himself a physician."
Hippocrates (born c. 460 BC)

Hippocrates, the fifth century BC Greek physician and 'father of medicine' and supposed author of the Hippocratic Oath, maintained that no one should be allowed to practise medicine who had not first studied astrology. Another Greek physician, Claudius Galen, brought together a huge range of knowledge and ideas in the second century AD which dominated medical practice until the 17th century. Among his teachings was a diagnostic technique which assumed that illnesses and their treatments were affected by and governed by the phases of the Moon. For centuries, astrology was a compulsory component of medical training (and still is in some natural medicine degrees), albeit only one aspect of diagnosis and treatment.

Medical or health astrology concerns particular ways of determining and interpreting an individual's horoscope with particular reference to health issues - diagnosis of current dis-eases, identification of areas of bodily weaknesses, and the prescription of natural cures and remedies. In ancient times, and still even today, the movement of the stars and planets was believed to affect bodily functions, and to cause ailments, or cure them.

During the Middle Ages, many drawings of the 'zodiac man' were made, which showed which signs of the zodiac were related to each part of the body, providing information as to the best times of the year to undertake cures for ailments affecting the corresponding body parts.

Health astrology persists today in many forms and among astrologers themselves, from whom clients seek counsel on health-related issues, and while it certainly cannot be used diagnose a condition or dis-ease, one's Sun sign, along with other factors of the natal chart, can definitely indicate potential problem areas of weakness or possible troubles. This branch of astrology has been found to be surprisingly accurate in most cases. While mostly accurate, none of the following information should ever be used as a substitute for professional medical advice should you be personally concerned about any of the conditions or afflictions listed for your Sun sign.

SAGITTARIAN HEALTH

"Jupiter natures rebel against confinement, and too much of it can bring on serious illness. If the Sagittarian can survive that, and the wear and tear of scattering his energies, he'll live to be as old as Methuselah. Most Archers retain their faculties, razor sharp and refined by age, to the end. Senility is almost never a problem."
Linda Goodman

Sagittarius is associated with the Hips, Thighs, Liver, Sciatic Nerves, Pelvis, Blood, Loins, Femur, Femoral Artery, Blood Vessels, Iliac Nerves, Coccyx Vertebrae, Ischium, Occipital Lobe, Sacral Region, Gluteus Muscles, and the Production of Gall.

Typical Sagittarians are usually healthy and energetic, and their optimistic outlook ensures they usually recover quickly from any illness, as well as keeping them strong in mind if sickness strikes. The hips, thighs, nerves and arteries are under the rule of Sagittarius, and its subjects may suffer rheumatism in the lower legs, as well as sciatica, pelvic disorders, jaundice, gout and nervous disorders. The lungs and throat may also be delicate, and Sagittarians may be prone to bronchitis and lung troubles. Sagittarians often suffer from hips and leg conditions or accidents - the commonest accidents suffered by Sagittarians are those affecting the lower limbs, dislocation of the hip and fracture of the thigh - the whole range of arthritic and rheumatic problems, and of course their tendency to be clumsy and therefore trip over or collide with things. Sports and outdoor adventure injuries and afflictions are also very likely. Asthma and other conditions and allergies picked up from animals, are also linked with Sagittarius, being an animal-lover.

Sagittarius represents the energy of movement and freedom. Your nature is dry, hot and expansive. Principal rulerships include the buttocks, sacrum, coordination of muscles, locomotion, pancreas (blood sugar levels), and autonomic nervous system (fight-or-flight/digest/relax).

The typical Sagittarian needs constant contact with a wide variety of people and experiences to keep himself in good health. Your nervous system is highly strung and keenly adapted to respond to the joys and freedoms of outdoor activity. You must keep on the go - visiting, organising, participating, leading, discussing, exchanging. Any prolonged curtailment or restraint is likely to be damaging to your spirit, and in turn, your health. They could even lead to breakdowns.

You have above average resistance to most diseases, which is not surprising seeing you are the great wanderer of the zodiac. You are very rarely incapacitated with serious afflictions, but on the rare occasions when you do have to stay in bed, you soon become restless and distressed.

Your longevity is one of the best in the zodiac, provided you don't burn yourself out with speedy, reckless pursuits or careless, thrill-seeking activities. You need to temper your use of energy reserves and take care not to over-extend yourself to the point of exhaustion. You often don't make the best of your vitality, as you have a habit of scattering your energies in ways that produce very little that is worthwhile, purposeful, substantial or productive.

You love physical, active sports and adventure, which gives you a greater tendency to injure, strain and over-exert yourself. Overall however, you have an inborn robustness and strong physical constitution - and you certainly need it to keep up the vigorous pace at which you live. A great believer in tomorrow, you are also helped by an extremely optimistic attitude toward life. Being so good-natured and cheerful helps to keep you fit on all levels.

Your ruling planet Jupiter is associated with the Blood, Arterial System, Pleura, Right Ear, Liver, Hips, Thighs, Arteries, Semen, Lungs, Varicose Veins, Nerve Sheaths, Glycogen, Suprarenals, Blood Fibrin, Upper Forehead, and the Disposal and

Dispersal of Body Fats. It is also connected with the Pituitary Gland, which regulates hormone production and bodily growth. Jovial Jupiter's influence upon Sagittarius is also likely to indicate health problems arising from over-indulgence in food and alcohol. Biliousness is highly likely if your diet is not watched carefully. Jupiterian conditions may arise if you indulge in a careless or indulgent lifestyle, such as high cholesterol, serum problems, liver issues, pleurisy, obesity, diabetes, stroke, high blood pressure, sciatica, hip and thigh problems, gout and general stress.

Keeping yourself in excellent health overall, with a special awareness of Sagittarius' vulnerable points, is key to achieving all you set out to do, and getting the most out of your life!

THE CELL SALTS ★ ASTROLOGICAL TONICS

Homeopathy and astrology have colluded to provide a wonderful list of astrological tonics, one particularly suited to each of the twelve signs. These are called 'homeopathic cell salts', 'tissue salts' or 'biochemic cell salts', and are available in most health food stores, are inexpensive and easy to take. They are considered to be gentle, effective and safe, even for children, people in fragile health states, and the elderly. Although the full picture, drawn from a full natal horoscope, gives a fuller, more accurate idea of an individual's unique constitution, even simply working with one's date of birth can be enough for the medical astrologer to suggest the use of a cell salt based upon the correlation with an individual's Sun sign. As well as the cell salts having a significant effect upon physical ailments, they can also profoundly influence the subtle energy bodies, including the mental, emotional, etheric and spiritual. Although the most common use of these salts is based upon each salt's correspondence with a Sun sign, use of the cell salt related to one's Moon sign can assist with addressing deeper underlying emotional issues, such as anxiety, depression, panic and fear. Use of the cell salt relating to your Moon sign will therefore help to restore your sense of safety, balance, security and emotional resilience. In the first seven years of life, when the Moon is the most influential sphere in our lives, Lunar cell salts are the most appropriate choice as a remedy or tonic.

For specific health problems, take both the salt of your Sun or Moon sign, *and* the salt that pertains to the specific condition. The same principle applies to the Ascendant sign, as the First House represents one's physical health, and especially if the Sun or Moon is a rising planet, which means rulership of the whole chart. For the purposes of this book, however, the cell salt that correlates with your Sun sign only is outlined.

TISSUE SALT FOR SAGITTARIUS ★ SILICA

Silicon Dioxide, or Silica, is the cell salt for Sagittarius. Present in the body in only trace amounts, it is vital to bone development, dental health, cartilage flexibility, and the health of connective tissues and the skin. Found mainly in connective tissues, the epidermis and the brain, Silica helps to build hair, skin and nails. Used for fatigue, oversensitivity to noises, greater mental strength, absentmindedness, crankiness, nervous exhaustion, hair loss, mucous congestion, body odour, pus formation, stomach pains, weak nails and many other related conditions, Silica is referred to as the 'homeopathic surgeon' due to its ability to assist the body to throw off non-functional organic matter. It is of use whenever there is pus that needs to be discharged, such as that found in abscesses, boils or splinters. Taking Silica after surgery helps to reduce scar formation, as well as helping the body expel foreign objects such as splinters and stitches. It is indicated for all injuries and slow-healing wounds, as well as all septic conditions in the body. As Sagittarius rules the liver, sciatic nerve, hips, thighs, and the autonomic nervous system, Sagittarians who are under stress tend to use up their Silica, leaving them more susceptible to chronic problems involving liver function or hip degeneration as they age. A basic nutrient for the hair, skin, teeth and nails, this remedy cleanses and eliminates waste, with a slow but deep and long-lasting effect on the body. Silica is found in such food sources as oats, cucumber, onions, wheat, figs, barley, rye, asparagus, parsnips, horseradish, rice, strawberries, cherries, cabbage, and most fruit and vegetable skins.

FIRE SIGN SAGITTARIUS & THE CHOLERIC HUMOR

Greek physician Hippocrates (460 - 370 BC) theorised that certain human behaviours were caused by body fluids, called 'humours'. Later, Galen of Pergamon (AD 131 - 200), a Greek physician, developed the first typology of temperaments to encompass many facets of the human psyche and physiology. These also related to the classical elements of Fire, Earth, Air and Water - as choleric, melancholic, sanguine and phlegmatic respectively. According to the Greeks who developed the temperament theory (the word stems from the Latin word *temperamentum*, meaning mixture), temperament is the 'mixture' of qualities that combine to form elements in physics and humours in medicine. The Greeks sought equilibrium in the four qualities of hot, cold, wet (moist), and dry, the elements of Earth, Air, Fire and Water, and the four humours of choler or yellow bile, melancholer or black bile, blood and phlegm. If balance was achieved, the person was said to be well- or even-tempered, and the importance of determining the temperament allowed for imbalances to be treated.

In ancient times, each of the four types of humours corresponded to a different personality type, which were associated with a domination of various biological functions. It was suggested that the temperaments came to clearest manifestation in childhood, between around the ages of six and fourteen of age, after which they become subordinate, but still influential, factors in our personality. It is important to note that your temperament is not your personality. However, your personality can incorporate parts of the temperament in its expression. Personality is shaped by both external and internal factors, whereas the temperament is innate, an inborn, inherent part of each individual.

The Fire element corresponds with the humour choleric, which is characterised by a short response time-delay, but response sustained for a relatively long time. Driven by their goals, for which they will use others as tools to achieve them, a choleric disposition represents touchiness, restlessness, aggression, spirit, excitement, changeability, impulsiveness, activity and optimism.

Choleric is associated with the ego level of self. Its taste is salty and sour, its nature acidic, its indication yellow bile. The choleric humour is associated with the astral body ^ *, and with hot and dry conditions.

---

^ A couple of thousand years ago, the Mesopotamians, Chinese and Egyptians, and more recently the Arabs, practised a medicine called 'of three bodies'. According to the doctors of the ancient world (who often practised as astrologers as well), a human being had three bodies: the physical body, the ethereal (or vital) body and the astral body, imparting a holistic approach to health. In modern medicine, usually only the physical body is focused upon fully. According to tradition, this physical body comprises three principles or states corresponding to three primordial elements: *solid* (Earth), *liquid* (Water) and *gas* (Air). This is the material body, the physical outer cover of muscles, nerves and organs held together by the skeleton. The Fire element corresponds with the *astral* body, which sits outside the physical body in one's auric field.

* The primordial element linked to the astral body is Fire, and it includes seven points, or doors, of perception which correspond exactly with the chakras. The astral body has a degree of vibration and radiance which is far higher than that of the ethereal body, an area which sits just beyond the physical body in one's auric field. Ancient physicians believed that this radiance covered an area varying from 40 centimetres to three metres around the physical body, and that this area varied greatly depending on the psychic energy of the individual. (The higher the levels, the larger the area of the radiance). The astral body is described as a diffused outer layer with whirls and flashing swirls of colour which move constantly. The intensity of its colour and movement varies according to the pattern of thoughts, feelings, emotions, moods and desires of the individual.

MONEY ATTRIBUTES

Colour for Increased Earning Power ★ Royal Blue

The following plants can be used by all zodiac signs to assist in attracting money ★ Ginger, Allspice, Clover, Orange, Marjoram, Cinnamon, Sassafras, Woodruff, Bergamot, Tonka Beans, Heliotrope, Alfalfa, Coltsfoot, Thyme, Mace, Irish Moss, Clove, Almond, Corn, Honeysuckle, Sesame, Nutmeg, Vetiver, Poppy, Jasmine, Dill and Elder Flower. To attract luck and success, try using any of the above, combined with any of the following: Alfalfa Seeds, Basil, Mustard Seeds, Vervain Leaves, Poppy Seeds, Rosemary, Lemon, Anise and Holly.

Striving for financial gain and abundance with a healthy inner moral compass is, in my view, one of the most noble goals we can set for ourselves. When we have more money, we are better placed to help ourselves and of course others; after all, as Abraham Maslow's Hierarchy of Needs model (1943) attests, once our primary and base survival needs have been satisfied, we can then advance higher towards loftier achievements, such as self-confidence, creativity and self-actualisation. Prosperity allows us to turn our attention to these more transcendental matters - to reach for lives not just of material comfort and luxuries, but of meaning, generosity, balance, harmony, fulfilment and joy. Our Sun sign can offer clues as to how we go about acquiring, earning, saving, maintaining, and allowing the overall flow of giving and receiving money. What's *your* money style?

You aim to acquire wealth and you often succeed. You are interested in financial security but often try to hide this in the offhand, careless manner in which you treat money. More than most, you are attracted to gambling, get-rich-quick schemes or big ideas, but you will be luckier in all things monetary if you follow a single course of action and avoid speculative risks (even if you *are* the luckiest sign of the zodiac when it comes to spinning the dice). You should definitely not allow yourself to become overly optimistic or idealistic in money matters, as although your ruling planet Jupiter endows you with much spontaneous luck, you tend to drift along thinking (and hoping) your luck will change. This only serves to make you directionless and lacking in true purpose and meaning, which is a waste of your intelligence on a grand scale. Perhaps your luck *will* change, but you should never assume that it will. And as saving is not one of your virtues, you will have nothing to fall back on should you fall from your cloud.

You love money for the freedom it allows you, but it slips through your fingers easily as you become bored with mundane financial matters and don't bother to educate yourself on the nitty gritty down-to-Earth dynamics of money. Naturally extravagant, you enjoy money when you have some and run up huge debts when you don't. A born gambler, you tend to leave financial planning to chance, rarely looking at bank statements. Being innately trusting, you are easily drawn in to get-rich-schemes. You are, however, naturally lucky at attracting money and wealth through your innately optimistic outlook and careless attitude towards finances, which seems to paradoxically draw money to you.

Money is important to you, mainly because of the adventure and freedom that it can 'buy', and you often spend lavishly, on impulse, and thoughtlessly. Usually willing to save up for certain things, you are often lucky in that money comes to you freely. You are forever trying to widen your financial horizons in whatever means possible. Being an independent spirit and the eternal freedom-seeker, you love that money can indeed buy you the lifestyle you desire - and that, to you, is the ultimate freedom.

COLOURS

Chromatomancy, or divination by colour, is a form of energy therapy that has been used for thousands of years by many different cultures. It works on the principle that we make both instinctive and rational choices or preferences based on circumstances which are already present in ourselves; colour also has an effect on the energy in an environment, and we in turn respond consciously or subconsciously to our surroundings. If we look at the causes, and try to understand the reasons, as to why we are so receptive to one particular colour over another, we will see that there is a subtle link between certain hues and our emotional and instinctive individual reactions. The colour which we give to things results from a combination of three elements:

1. The light or the vibration of a body;

2. The context in which it is found and the interaction between its own light and that of its environment;

3. The sensitivity of the eye's retina which sees the body in question. Because of this, a colour can vary, depending on the individual's perceptions, namely, his sensitivity, his mood, and his view of reality. For a long time, people have understood that their vision of reality depends a lot on their moods, feelings and emotions.

Chromatotherapy, or colour healing, stems from this body of evidence, and its main application is the use of colours for healing purposes. Colours are generally associated with characteristics, feelings, stones, metals, plants and flowers, planets and even the zodiac signs. In varying cultures, they play a significant role in ceremonies and regalia.

We vibrate to the frequency of colour, shown through its continual movement and change in our aura ^. One of the most beautiful examples of colour is the rainbow. This architect of colour is caused by the refraction and internal reflection of light in raindrops. Colour can be perceived as either a pigment, or as illumination. The colour spectrum can be divided into eight main colours: red, orange, yellow, green, turquoise, blue, violet and magenta. Each colour has a wavelength and frequency that carry different therapeutic qualities which have indirect effects upon our health and bodily systems, and because of this, coupled with the fact that we as living energy centres emanate colour, colour can be a great medium in healing, calming, energising, increasing and attracting.

Aristotle, in the fourth century BCE, considered blue and yellow to be the true primary colours and related them to life's polarities: Sun and Moon, male and female, stimulation and sedation, in and out, expansion and contraction. He also associated colours with the four elements of Fire, Earth, Air and Water. Hippocrates, the father of medicine, used colour extensively in medicinal healing and recognised that the therapeutic effects of a white violet differed from those of a purple one. In the fifteenth century, Paracelsus placed particular importance on the role of colour in healing.

Each Sun sign and planetary body has a specific colour or colours which when used in combination with wishing rituals, can enhance their power immensely. Coloured candles can be used to good effect, as the fire energy of the flame/s increases the power of any wish, and flames are also a useful aid to meditating on, focusing upon or clarifying what you want. Coloured candles help to focus the energy for whatever purpose the colour is in sympathy with (e.g. green for money, pink for romance, orange for joy, etc.)

With all this in mind, wearing or using your Sun sign or ruling planet's magical colour/s on a regular basis will undoubtedly bring great benefits.

^ The aura is defined as an energy field, which interpenetrates with, and radiates beyond, the physical body. Clairvoyantly seen, the aura is full of light, colour and shade. The trained healer or seer sees or senses indications within the aura as to the spiritual, physical and emotional state of the individual. Much of the auric colour and energy emanates from the chakras.

YOUR LUCKY COLOURS

For Sagittarius ★ Purple, Deep Royal Blue, Indigo, Orange, Yellow, Green, Rich Purple, Mauve

For Jupiter ★ Azure*, Purple, Turquoise, Blue, Indigo, Gold, Yellow

* 'Azure' is from the Arabic for Lapiz Lazuli, the amazingly brilliant blue gemstone. It is used to describe the colour blue, particularly when it symbolises royalty. This was particularly so with heraldry, where blue is also represented by the planet Jupiter, your ruler.

Being the most sophisticated of the Fire signs and ruled by Jupiter, Sagittarians reflect this by being drawn to the colours purple and dark royal blue.

Each of the eight colours of the rainbow spectrum also has a complementary colour to which it is matched. Red is complementary to turquoise, orange to blue, yellow to violet, and green to magenta. If these colour pairs enhance each other's most spellbinding qualities and energies, perhaps you could try wearing your Sun sign's lucky colour with its matching complementary colour in order to produce extra magical results! Your lucky Sagittarian colours are purple, turquoise - which is complemented by red - and (royal) blue - which is complemented by orange. Now you know your colours, you can dress for success!

FEATURE COLOURS ★ PURPLE, TURQUOISE & BLUE

★ PURPLE ★

"When I am an old woman I shall wear purple."
Jenny Joseph

Planetary Associations ★ Uranus, Jupiter, the Moon

Healing Qualities ★ Powerful, Psychic, Beautiful, Awareness, Inspiring, High Ideals, Wisdom, Protective, Spiritual Awareness, Creativity

Keywords ★ Problem-solving, Intuitive, Psychic Realm, Resurrection, Royalty (red + blue), Spiritual Power, Dignity, Piety, Creativity, Uranus, the Moon, Truth, the Cosmos

The colour of Uranus and of the element of ether or spirit, purple may also be used to represent the Moon's power in healings. It is the last visible colour before ultraviolet, so it is often associated with time, space and the Universe itself. Purple is an intriguing colour because it combines and balances the diametrically opposed attributes of two colours: the fire and passion of red, and the coolness and calm of blue. This quality makes purple both an exciting and thought-provoking colour that elicits mixed reactions, able to imply either greater wisdom or underlying confusion. Despite this conflict, it has been said that more than three quarters of children prefer this shade to any other. It can enhance ambition, astral work, compassion, psychic abilities, spirituality, and improve luck and spiritual love. A colour of transformation at a deep level, purple denotes spiritual peace and awareness. Purple crystals such as amethyst and purple jade, are associated with realisation and illumination, and as such are perfect stones for those wishing to succeed; purple gems can be used to attract good fortune into your life. Lighter shades of purple, such as lilac and lavender, evoke gentle feelings of romance, comfort and nostalgia, and the warmth of pale purple is less striking than that of other bright shades such as pink and orange, because it is tempered with the coolness of blue. Striking a balance between the two, purple can therefore be soft and atmospheric, suggesting distance and aloofness, or whimsical and full of fancy, the colour of first love and of devotion. The blue and red elements within purple also symbolise powerful fusion of the celestial and the Earthly. Pale purples are connected to spiritual enlightenment, to the Third Eye and to contacting the spirit world. You can use purples to provide protective energy and enhance your strength and psychic abilities. It is associated with the Crown chakra, the link between yourself and Nirvana, or complete enlightenment and, when balanced, will render you happy, contented and fulfilled. Purple in Feng Shui is associated with the Fire element and is linked with the south and with determination, joy and inner Fire. As the colour of the south, it is connected with the desire for fame, status and recognition. Purple is the colour of mystery and nobility, merging the tranquillity of blue with the heat and boldness of red. Because it combines the energy and vitality of red with the stability of blue, it is the perfect colour to stimulate the mind while keeping stress at bay; shades of purple have been shown to help calm people with nervous or mental imbalances. A very spiritual and relaxing colour, its connections with opulence, nobility, dignity, power and wealth stretch back to ancient times, when it was believed to have been Cleopatra's favourite colour; and in Ancient Rome, a crimson substance was first extracted from molluscs and then used to create a purple dye that coloured the ornate garments of the emperors. It can stimulate your imagination, or inspire you and improve your creativity. People who are drawn to this colour often have an interest in spiritual growth. During the sixties, the colour purple was considered unconventional and rebellious, and came to symbolise the decade's search for freedom and a more Universal concept of love. Overall, purple is a common colour in magic; a purple candle represents Uranus, Jupiter and the power of the Moon; it can be used to enhance luck or telepathy, while a purple 'spell' bag can be used for protection and healing. The herb and colour lavender is also an essential ingredient in any ritual or magical work, being used to make wishes, attract your soul mate or for healing spells. Purple magic is, in essence, potent, mystical and unique.

★ TURQUOISE ★

Planetary Association ★ Jupiter

Healing Qualities ★ Refreshing, cleansing, calming but invigorating, uplifting, creative, open communication, clarity of thought, inner healing through empathy

Complementary Colour ★ Red or Orange

Turquoise is a colour of Jupiter and can represent Air and the sky. It is a variation of the colour blue, and is derived by mixing together blue and green. It can veer towards either of these colours but is best known as possessing a vibrant, opaque bright bluish tone. This vivid colour, reminiscent of a tropical ocean, is both invigorating and calming. It promotes emotional balance and stability, recharging our spirits during times of mental stress and fatigue. As the spiritual stone of the Native Americans and the Aztecs, turquoise symbolises truth and aids communication on all levels. It indicates a dynamic quality of being, a highly energised personality, positive influence over others, and the ability to project oneself to beneficial effect - great for getting those brilliant ideas across! Good for heightening creativity and sensitivity, it helps to sharpen our powers of observation and perception. Turquoise is a wonderful all-round healer and general tonic for the immune system. It is ultimately the colour of calm, serenity and spiritual harmony.

★ BLUE ★

Planetary Associations ★ The Sun *, Venus

* Blue is said to be the true colour of the Sun

Complementary Colour ★ Orange

Healing Qualities ★ Soothing, Clarity, Calming, Protective, Mental Control, Sedative, Communication, Productivity, Purifying

Keywords ★ Healing, Tranquillity, Thoughtfulness, Peace, Calmness, Water, Venus, The Sky, Truth,

Turquoise and blue, and their respective complementary rainbow spectrum colours red and orange, as well as purple, are Sagittarius's special LUCKY colours! They can be worn or otherwise used together to dazzling and mesmerising effect.

SAGITTARIUS' CHAKRA CORRESPONDENCE ★ THE THIRD EYE

The word 'chakra' comes from the Sanskrit and means 'wheel', disc' or 'circle'. Chakras are vitally important to your physical health, emotional wellbeing and spiritual growth, and are regarded as a complete integrated system that works holistically. The chakras are funnel-shaped spinning energy vortexes of multi-coloured light. These swirling vortexes of energy absorb and distribute life-force, the subtle energy known as *prana*. The seven master chakras - Root, Sacral, Solar Plexus, Heart, Throat, Third Eye and Crown - lie in the centre line of the body, with the first five embedded within the spinal column. Each chakra vibrates at a different vibrational frequency and on a different note, and responds to specific life issues or 'thought forms'.

The lower body chakras deal with physical issues. As we move up the body, the chakras correspond to increasingly spiritual concerns. As a consequence, each chakra's energy vibrates at a different rate, depending on whether they govern earthbound or ethereal issues. The lower chakras have slower and denser vibrations, while the higher chakras spin at faster speeds with higher vibrations.

Because the chakras have no physical manifestation and cannot be located using any scientific instrument, they have tended to be viewed with scepticism by many Western medical professionals, a distinction they share with energy points in acupuncture and the notion of meridians. Instead, they are believed to have been sensed intuitively by many people over many centuries, and indeed people in yoga positions and in deep meditation have reported experiencing the sensation of a surge of energy rising from the base of the spine and emerging through the top of the head. Some people have even said they have seen points of blue light when their *kundalini* energy has risen from the lowest chakra to the highest, as well as experiencing a profound sense of happiness and ecstasy.

In summary, the Universal Life Force enters the body through the Crown chakra at the top of the head. As it works its way through the body, it flows through the other centres. As it spreads to the Base chakra, it is said to arouse the kundalini energy, which yogis believe sleeps in a coiled serpentine form.

The chakra associated with Sagittarius is the sixth, or Third Eye chakra, which governs spiritual sight, Divine connections, intuition, psychic vision, wisdom and clairvoyance.

THIRD EYE CHAKRA

Location ★ Between the Physical Eyes
Colour ★ Dark Blue/Indigo
Concerned with ★ Clairvoyance, Wisdom, Intuition & Vision

Gland ★ Pineal
Essential Oils ★ Basil, Angelica Seed, Carrot Seed, Clove Bud, Clary Sage, Ginger, Melissa, Peppermint, Black Pepper
Animal ★ Owl
Shape ★ Downward Triangle
Element ★ Light, Avyakta
Planets ★ Jupiter, Neptune
Zodiac Signs ★ Sagittarius, Pisces
Flower ★ Two-petalled Lotus
Energy State ★ Imagery
Mantra ★ OM

Positive Expression ★ Spiritually wise, intuitive, personal awareness of the Divine

Negative Expression (Blockage) ★ Too self-sufficient, lack of imagination, vision or concentration, clouded intuition, inability to see the bigger picture, delusional, distorted imagination or intuition, over-reliance on logic and intellect

The Third Eye chakra is located between and just above the physical eyes. Its Sanskrit name is *Anja*, and its symbol is two large white lotus petals on each side of a white circle, within which is a downward-pointing triangle. Balance in this chakra is expressed as developed and sound senses of intuition, clairvoyance, clairaudience and clairsentience. It corresponds to the pituitary gland and the carotid nerve plexus. Crystals that can be used to cleanse and balance this chakra are mostly indigo, deep blue and purple stones such as: Lapis Lazuli, Amethyst,

Azurite, Charoite, Lepidolite, Sugilite, Azeztulite, Turquoise, Iolite, Larimar, Blue Calcite, Moldavite, Angelite, Phenacite, Tanzanite and Purple Fluorite.

LUCKY CAREER TIPS & PATHS THAT WILL MAKE YOUR BANK BALANCE & SPIRITUAL SELF SOAR

The branch of astrology known as 'vocational astrology' encompasses the areas of one's calling, career path, or ideal profession. Careers, jobs, professions and occupations can all mean different things to different people, but to simplify the definition, I refer to a vocation as one's true calling, one's authentic path, and a dynamic way of life which pays an income in some form and leads to a deep fulfilment of personal and spiritual needs. An ideal vocation will provide self-fulfilment, ego satisfaction, and feed one's inner drive to achieve what they ultimately wish to achieve, whether that be to gain recognition, wealth or approval, to travel, to learn and fulfil an inner need for knowledge, an urge to serve others in some way, or an urge to improve personal, societal or Universal conditions.

In order to gain ultimate fulfilment and self-esteem, we all need a purpose in life. Many people gain this through their work, providing the job or career they choose suits their temperament, talents and aspirations. If our professional life is unsatisfactory or disharmonious in any way, frustration, unhappiness and even despair can result. Although your whole horoscope would need to be drawn up and interpreted in order to gain more substantial, deeper insights into your ideal career and purpose, you can begin by being guided by your Sun sign, which can give you many pointers to a suitable, and therefore successful, career path. You just never know, something in the following might jump out at you and make your soul dance immediately - and hopefully all the way to the bank!

> "Many Sagittarians seek the stage and no one is happier giving encore after encore for an excited audience. He'll sing himself hoarse or dance his shoes off for the sheer exhilaration of performing. Show business is full of Archers."
> **Linda Goodman**

With your Sun in Sagittarius, you are cheerful, hopeful, idealistic, generous, sunny and sociable. A natural teacher and mentor, you pass on knowledge in any way you can, and always give it with a generous heart. As your desire for worldly success is strong, you may change careers midstream if it suits your ever-changing needs and thoughts. Adaptable, versatile and with a great love of novelty and stimulation, boredom and repetition will repel you, so it would be wise to choose a profession which satisfies you need for newness, variety and fresh ideas and faces. Your ideal vocation gives you freedom, variety, and mental and social invigoration.

As a typical Sagittarian, you also enjoy working outdoors, in nature or with animals. Basically optimistic and outgoing, you also need freedom and independence, so it is imperative that you have room to move in any career path - mentally, physically, spiritually, emotionally *and* financially. Flexibility and adaptability to change are your fortes.

Ideal careers for Sagittarius are: Freelance Anything, Professor, Lecturer, Teacher, Lawyer, Athlete, Barrister, Foreign Affairs, Philosopher, Veterinary Surgeon, Explorer, Travel Agent, Public Speaker, Animal Breeder, Horse Trainer, Sportsperson, Jockey, Priest, Faith Healer, Poet, Publisher, Bookseller, Judge, Magistrate, Writer and Librarian.

As a rule, and by your nature, Sagittarians usually cannot and will not undertake dull, monotonous or routine work. You love to advance yourself by learning, studying and challenging yourself. Your ambitions must have positive expression and to be tied to a desk or a boring nine to five job would be worse than anything your expansive, seeking mind could possibly imagine.

You will instinctively be drawn towards and excel in fields which expand the mind and broaden horizons or relations such as Tourism, Trekking, Voyaging, Exploring, Discovering, Foreign Correspondence, Literature, Astronomy, Metaphysics, Overseas Travel, Religion, the Shipping Industry, Seafaring, Sailing, and the scientific community. You also have a flair for Drama, Flamboyance, Artful Expression and Theatrics, so a career in show business could well be your calling.

The Archer naturally gravitates to most sporting or outdoor professions, and for this reason you are suited to Travel, Exploration, Adventure and Hunting. Additionally, the urge to spread your wings and fly (sometimes literally) means you will lean towards expanding your prospects in any way possible.

You are on an eternal quest for knowledge, so you may moonlight as an avid reader or university student studying for a degree. At other times, you may lack direction and drift aimlessly, but your ruling planet Jupiter endows you with enough luck for something to fall into your lap eventually. You are also blessed with enough intelligence to spot these opportunities when they land, and will take up most job offers if they offer stimulation and enough leeway for any simultaneous side interests you have going on at any one time.

Because Sagittarians have broad vision and are far-sighted, you are often looking ahead into the future and enjoy forecasting; in this way you possess more vision and imagination than most of the other zodiac signs (with the exception of perhaps the idealistic, futuristic Aquarius). Also clever with words, you naturally understand the law and its mechanics and intricacies, making a good lawyer or barrister, or perhaps even a judge or magistrate.

With your innate love of ideas, religion and philosophies, you would also make a fine Priest, Minister or Spiritual Healer. You have the power to influence others, but are prone to arrogance and self-righteousness at times, which can undermine your messages somewhat.

You are a good gambler and think little of taking risks, often making successful business deals, but you do not like dealing with the finer details, preferring to travel and spread goodwill for your company, field or business partner.

Generally full of enthusiasm, high spirits and energy, it would be fatal to your free spirit to find yourself in a vocation which is dreary, detailed, ordinary, staid, slow-moving or uninspiring. Above all else, you love to be active and to feel moved by everything you undertake. Shake it up!

LUCKY PLACES WHERE YOUR ENERGY IS HEIGHTENED

As the Fire element and Choleric humour corresponds with hot and dry conditions, warm, arid and low-humidity places suit your constitution, disposition and temperament. The following nations, countries and cities are also locations whose vibrations are closely allied with the sign of Sagittarius: Saudi Arabia, Barbados, Chile, Madagascar, Santo Domingo, India, Prague, Australia (Sydney), Singapore, China, Kazakhstan, Spain, South Africa, Germany (Stuttgart), Toronto, Italy (Tuscany), the Australian outback, Bangladesh, Hungary and Ireland. Bhutan, Kenya, Lebanon, Anguilla, Mauritania, The Netherlands, Central African Republic, Benin, Tanzania, Mayotte, Surinam and The Yemen are also in tune with the Sagittarian energy, as are anywhere foreign, well-known universities and grand libraries, and upper rooms with fireplaces. Any extravagant adventure holiday that feeds your need for adventure, a road trip across Wild West America with an obligatory stop at Las Vegas and the Grand Canyon, visits to some of the world's famous universities, religious temples and libraries, a drive along Australia's famous Nullarbor Plain (to appeal to your freedom and love of wide, open spaces), or a desert trek on horseback (think Central Australia or Saudi Arabia) or somewhere exotic, where the climate is hot and dry (while you are there at least!) and that offers plenty of opportunities for you to delve into the region's history, philosophies, religions, culture and learning or legal institutions, could very well be your ticket to Sagittarian heaven!

GEMS & CRYSTALS

"People love stones, and apparently stones love people. Like the angels they may be, they seem endlessly willing to serve the wellbeing of humans and to help us achieve our desires …Unlike people of the ancient past, we now have access to virtually the entire mineral kingdom. We have the opportunity to work like modern alchemists, combining and arranging the stones and their currents, looking for combinations and patterns that can help us enhance our inner and outer lives."

Robert Simmons, *Stones of the New Consciousness*

Each crystal and mineral of the Earth embodies different qualities, patterns or potential expressions of the Divine language, the silent whispers of the Universe. If we can accept the fact that the human body is a sophisticated, multi-faceted antenna system comprised of a crystalline matrix that is constantly transmitting and receiving all manner of energies, it could then be assumed that energy and body workers who use quartz, shells and stones, which are also crystalline materials, have the power to promote resonant interactions with the liquid 'crystal' structures found in human tissues. It could even be said that we are all made of essentially the same substances and structures, and that crystals and gemstones vibrate at varying energetic levels which can connect with our own in order to 'buzz' and dance together to make a harmonious Uni-verse both within and without.

All crystals work through vibrational balancing and by channelling energy. The magic of crystals is in their colour, which is determined by the rate at which their atoms vibrate; these vibrations can be matched to the energy given by your own body's aura. And just as light can be focused and refracted through gemstones, so too can all kinds of psychic energy, from healing energies to Divine communications.

Gemstones can help us attune to higher vibrations and bring them into our own experience and being. This theory of crystal resonance suggests that the characteristic energy patterns emanated by any stone can be transferred into the 'liquid crystal medium' of our bodies through resonance. Our bodies, being composed of these tuneable liquids, can mimic and mirror any consistent vibrational pattern with which we come into contact; we can therefore resonate with the healthful qualities of various crystals and minerals.

Crystals and precious stones have been valued throughout world cultures over many centuries for their healing virtues and capacities to imbue courage, strength, invulnerability, clairvoyance, love and numerous other qualities. Wearing gemstones is one of the simplest and most effective self-healing practices you can undertake, and wearing or carrying those stones whose vibrations correspond with the qualities you wish to embody brings their energetic currents into engagement with your body.

Over time the phenomenon of energetic integration, may be felt tangibly and your own vibrational field may internalise the stone's currents and adjust to them and effectively 'store' them, making them, eventually, a part of your own vibrational make-up. And we seem to know from the resonances we feel within our bodies when in contact with these gemstones, that crystals emanate tangible, if oft immeasurable, currents.

Crystals act as transmitters and amplifiers of your will or intentions - as long as your will or intentions are in sympathy with the crystal's energy. The mineral kingdom refers to stones, minerals and crystals and the associations and vibrations they carry. When working with stones, we are working with several different layers of spiritual energies, and although they can be regarded as inanimate 'psychic batteries', they are actually moving, vibrating masses of energy which transmit potential and power into our lives. Some crystals and stones even have receptive powers, which means they can absorb energy and retain it within until cleansed or re-programmed.

Although it is untrue that the only stones you can usefully wear are the ones astrologically matched with your Sun sign or ruling planet, those which align with your Sun sign or ruling planet are your most fortuitous and therefore strongest 'attractors' and 'amplifiers'.

Twelve oracular gemstones were described in the Bible, as the author of *Exodus* (28-15 and 17-21) knew them. Yahweh spoke to Moses about the breastplate he would have to wear to train for priesthood, and described it to him in these words: "And thou shalt make the breastplate of judgement with cunning work; ... And thou shalt set in it settings of stones, even four rows of stones; the first row shall be a sardius, a topaz, and a carbuncle. And the second row shall be an emerald, a sapphire and a diamond. And the third row an opal, an agate and an amethyst. And the fourth row a beryl, and an onyx, and a jasper; they shall be set in hold in their inclosings. And the stones shall be with the children ... (all) twelve (of them)." Given that the compilers of the Bible lived during a time when astrological belief was prevalent in Babylon, it seems valid to assert that these previously named gemstones would have some astrological basis. Further, since these ancient people supposedly made correlations between each of the twelve precious stones, and one of the twelve zodiac signs, there are seven crystalline systems set down in crystallography (or the science of the laws which influence the formation, structure and geometric, physical and chemical properties of crystallised matter) as analogous with the seven traditional ruling planets of the zodiac.

However, nobody is under the rule of one planet alone. We are all in essence a complex mixture of every planet, many elements and varying aspects, depending on their positions, placements and prominence in our birth chart. Everything that goes on in the skies above us affects what is going on here on Earth, and also *within* us. Your lucky stones are to assist you to tune into your Sun sign's energy and planetary influences, but you are by no means limited to the ones listed for your sign alone. Above all, let your stones, whichever ones you choose, work for you and allow them to transport your very own unique and magical energy into the wider Universe.

> "Beautiful and strong is the material of stones, but more beautiful and much more powerful is the mystery that emanates from them."
> **Chinese Poet & Alchemist, Li Po, 8th Century A.D.**

★ CLEAR QUARTZ ★

The Master Healer ★ *For All Zodiac Signs*

A common, well-known and popular gem, clear quartz (sometimes known as rock crystal) is an all-purpose 'jack-of-all-trades' stone. It amplifies the magic of any work you do or wishes you make. It is connected with all the chakras and increases the power of all other crystals. Clear quartz is a deep soul cleanser, which unblocks and regulates energy and emotions on all levels. It is balancing and harmonising. In various cultures, quartz crystal is reputed to be the most powerful crystal, the 'grandfather crystal', and the 'chief of the Stone People'. Clear quartz is also considered to be the only gemstone that is modifiable to suit your needs *, as other crystals automatically contain and retain their own specific resonance or natural signature. In essence, clear quartz is the most easily programmable and the most overall healing and readily accessible crystals of the mineral kingdom, holding a unique importance in the Universe of gems. And because of its all-encompassing nature and wide-ranging healing abilities, it has zodiacal affinities with all the signs.

* To program your clear quartz crystal, simply hold it on your Third Eye chakra (between and just above the physical eyes) and concentrate on the purpose for which you wish to use it. Be positive and receptive while you allow your crystal to fill with this energy. If you wish, you could also state the intention of the programming out loud, for example, 'I program this crystal for love / healing / meditation / abundance / protection or (insert your own word here)'. You could also run your clear quartz crystal under running water, allow it to dry naturally, then hold the stone with both hands, bring it up to your mouth and blow into it sharply three times in order to impregnate it with your own breath. Then, hold it firmly in one hand and silently invite and welcome it into your life as a friend, helper and guide.

SAGITTARIAN & JUPITERIAN LUCKY CRYSTALS, STONES & GEMS

Sagittarius birth stones ★ Topaz, Turquoise, Zircon

November birth stones ★ Topaz, Citrine, Pearl

December birth stones ★ Ruby, Turquoise, Bloodstone, Lapis Lazuli, Zircon, Tanzanite (modern)

Topaz, Turquoise, Zircon (your three primary birthstones), Yellow Sapphire, Amethyst (Jupiter), Ruby, Bloodstone, Citrine, Pearl, Lapis Lazuli and Tanzanite (November and December birthstones) are your luckiest stones, and one or more of these gems should be worn about your person to ensure good luck and increase your magnetism. Dark Blue Spinel, Azurite, Labradorite, Obsidian, Smoky Quartz,

Lazurite, Blue Lace Agate, Dioptase, Gold Obsidian, Cyanite, Garnet, Okenite, Sodalite, Rhodochrosite, Charoite, Snowflake Obsidian, Malachite, Pink Tourmaline and Sugilite also align with Sagittarian energy.

CRYSTALS & THE PLANETS

All the Vedic texts agree in relating gems to planets. This verse from the *Jatax Parijat* links each gem to a planet:

'The ruby is the gem of the Lord of the Day (the Sun),
The shining pearl is the gem of the cold Moon,
Red coral is the gem of Mars,
The emerald is the gem of noble Mercury,
Yellow sapphire is the gem of Jupiter, instructor of gods,
Diamond is the gem of Venus, instructor of demons,
Blue sapphire is the gem of Saturn.'

Each planet influences its gem, and their curative power varies according to the position of its planet in the zodiac. Ayurvedic medicine has always paid attention to these details in their healing practices, often advising people to wear their corresponding zodiacal stone as a ring or a talisman.

CRYSTALS & THE ELEMENTS

Crystals are inextricably linked to the four elements, from their original creation to their potency and use in magical rituals and healing. Formed by the combination, in varying conditions, of different physical elements, such as metals, non-metals and gases, some stones require the enormous heat generated by volcanoes or deep thermal currents to bond their molecular makeup, while others may require pressure or water sources. The effects of the four elements of Fire, Earth, Air and Water is evident in these formation processes. The heat generated by Fire, pressure from the Earth, and the chemical reactions involved in absorbing elements from the Air and Water, all demonstrate the four elements in action to produce the correct conditions and ingredients necessary for the creation of crystals, lending them each their unique qualities.

CRYSTALS & THE FIRE ELEMENT

The transformational influence of Fire can be seen in such examples as citrine, which is formed when heat is applied to amethyst, and obsidian, which is created through astonishing volcanic temperatures. Although Fire can be a destructive force, its effect is also to change things, and it is this transformative energy which can be harnessed in Fire-inspired gemstones to help facilitate positive changes in your life, through meditation, chakra balancing or other magical rituals.

Some Fiery crystals are ★ Calcite, Ruby, Amber, Obsidian, Garnet, Citrine, Bloodstone (Heliotrope), Topaz, Spinel and Pyrite.

THE CRYSTALLINE SYSTEM OF YOUR RULING PLANET JUPITER

Associated with your traditional ruling planet Jupiter, are Amethyst, Beryl, Emerald, Sapphire and Turquoise. This is the fifth crystalline system, known as the rhomboidric system, that is having a parallelepiped whose six sides are diamond-shaped and of equal size, ideally represented by the Rhodochrosite or magnesium carbonate. This, it has been suggested, has a curative action on such Jupiterian afflictions as liver complaints, ulcers, asthma and congestion.

JUPITER'S GEMSTONE ASSOCIATION

★ **AMETHYST** ★ Connected with the Crown and Third Eye Chakras, this beautiful purple stone is used to aid and promote spiritual wisdom, intuition, protection, focus, inner peace, pleasant dreams, meditation, power, spiritual awareness, psychic abilities and healing. Calming, balancing and comforting, amethyst is a stone commonly used and worn by healers and spiritual workers, as it has the power to focus energies, brings forth 'unseen' realms, and heightens one's psychic perceptions. Purple has long been considered a royal colour, so it is not surprising that amethyst has been so revered and so much in demand throughout history. Amethysts are featured in the English Crown Jewels and were also a favourite of Ancient Egyptian royalty. Enchanted by the stone's energy, Leonardo da Vinci wrote that amethyst could dissipate evil thoughts and quicken the intelligence. It encompasses power, spirit, beauty and magic.

SAGITTARIUS'S FEATURE CRYSTAL ★ TOPAZ

A traditional stone of protection, topaz has long been believed to protect its wearer from harm. Usually orange-yellow or yellow-green in colour, topaz can also be found in blue, green, red, pink, yellow or colourless. It is believed that topaz originates from and bears the name of an island in the Red Sea off the coast of Egypt, which, according to legend, was plunged into thick fog day and night and solely inhabited by snakes. This island, known today as the Isle of St John, was infested with these snakes who were the guardians of the topaz. According to the legend, the flashes of these stones sparkling in the night gave a supernatural glow to the foggy island, and this famous luminosity which defied the dark forces of the night made the topaz gem a symbol of honesty, faith, purity, loyalty and righteousness. In ancient times amulets were made from topaz to protect the bearer from evil spirits or accidents, and it was believed that it changed colour to warn the bearer of imminent danger. The ancients also believed in its ability to arouse passions and intense feelings, to inspire enthusiasm and commitment, to regenerate the body, and to uncover acts of treachery and deceit, hence its connection and resonance with the zodiac sign of Scorpio also. African tribal people use it in their ceremonies to communicate with the spirit world and to attract and manifest both wealth and health.

Overall, it is an excellent stone to use for attraction and desire-drawing purposes, attracting people to you on friendship, love and business levels, and magnetising your desires as long as they are for the greater good. Topaz has the power to magnetise prosperity, honour, glory and recognition of your worth. This stone's vibrant energy brings abundance, generosity, joy, success and good fortune, and is particularly supportive for affirmations and manifestation. An empathetic stone that directs energy to where it is needed most, it soothes, heals, recharges, stimulates, remotivates, and aligns the meridians of the body. As well as promoting forgiveness and truth, it helps shed light upon one's path, tap into inner resources, and highlight goals. Eliminating doubt and uncertainty, topaz also encourages a sense of trust in the Universe, that enables you to simple *be* rather than *do*. This is an envisioning stone and helps you see the core of any issue. It has the capacity to see both the bigger picture and the minute detail, recognising how they interrelate. Excellent for cleansing the aura and for inducing relaxation, topaz (particularly golden, or imperial, topaz) acts like a battery and recharges spiritually and psychically, strengthening one's faith and optimism, reminding you of your Divine origins. With an affinity for the Sacral and Solar Plexus chakras, topaz encourages one to be benevolent in outlook and helps to promote a more selfless approach to life and be more considerate of the needs of others. It helps you discover your own inner wisdom and riches as well, making you feel confident and philanthropic and compelled to spread the good fortune and sunshine all around. As it can also reduce stress levels, it is a very useful stone for people involved in the caring professions or other stressful jobs. Encouraging relaxation and serenity, it is good for restoring calm and helping the mind to unwind. With its inherent protective properties, it is also effective in healing addictions and aiding detoxification - indeed, wearing a topaz crystal can give the immune system a boost and encourage it to cope with the difficulties of withdrawal. A piece of topaz can also be worn or carried when it feels like one's willpower is wavering, in any situation. An unusual characteristic of topaz is its apparent ability to puts its wearer in touch with life in other parts of the galaxy; it certainly can't hurt to try! As it enhances creativity, understanding and self-expression, topaz defines the essence of a true magic-worker; one who is courageous, a visionary, and filled with hope, inspiration and purpose.

SAGITTARIAN POWER CRYSTALS

Around six thousand years ago, in ancient Mesopotamia, the Sumerians started studying precious stones and minerals, as well as the stars, with a view of improving their lives in many ways by probing the secrets and mysteries of the Universe. Their esoteric interests and knowledge were such that they began to grasp the general connections between the Earth and the heavens, or the Solar system as they knew it, and the functions of stones and minerals as a link between the two. Their method of making these connections was by colour (for example the Sun was allocated all yellow stones), as well as other spiritual links. The gemstones listed for the portion of your zodiac sign are given their status as your 'power crystals' due to the links that can be made between your primary planetary ruler/s and your mutable planetary ruler (listed last), and each stone's particular colour, chemical and mineral compositions, healing properties, and the number they are given (based on the Mohs scale of hardness: for example, diamond scores a perfect 10 out of 10), all of which combine to align with your planetary rulers. Working mindfully with your planet's special crystals is one way you can increase the flow of power and magic into your life.

POWER CRYSTALS FOR FIRST HALF SAGITTARIANS ★ (22 November - 5 December)

Influenced by Jupiter and Mars

Watermelon Tourmaline (Melonstone), Phosphophylite, Amber, Eilat Stone, Aurichalcite, Chrysocolla

★ WATERMELON TOURMALINE ★

Watermelon tourmaline, combining pink and green colourings, is a powerful 'super-activator' of the Heart chakra, linking it to the higher self and fostering love, tenderness, healing and friendship. Watermelon tourmaline, when cut across its width, will show a pink centre surrounded by a green border, resembling a slice of watermelon, hence its name. Watermelon tourmaline in particular is good for easing distress and inducing relaxation. It is strongly protective, instils patience and teaches tact and diplomacy. It helps one to find the joy in situations, promotes inner security, alleviates depression and fear, and facilitates the understanding of situations and the ability to express one's intentions clearly. Working with the Heart, it benefits relationships, heals emotional dysfunction and releases old pain. Like all tourmalines, this stone contains unique positive and negative electrical properties which earned it its early name of the 'the mineral magnet' * (see under 'Tourmaline'); warmth also activates it, and it has long been associated with fire, electricity and magnetism. (See also under *'Power Crystals for Second Half Sagittarians: Tourmaline'*)

★ **AMBER** ★ Though not actually a stone (it is fossilised tree resin from an extinct form of pine that was submerged under the ocean many millions of years ago), amber is a powerful material to work with. It is one of the oldest materials used for jewellery, will attract pieces of paper when rubbed, and can generate an electrical charge when rubbed against cloth; many associate it with pure power for this reason. It is therefore effective in giving an extra energetic boost to any magical workings you may undertake. Amber has been celebrated in many ancient cultures as a bringer of courage and honesty and in China it was known as the 'Soul of the Tiger' and thought to protect against fire and water. In Ancient Rome, amber was given to gladiators for courage. Jewellery made from it has become increasingly popular in recent years, though it has been used by humans since the Stone Age. As well as its well-known yellow, orange or reddish-brown colour, amber is found in a range of other colours, including black, violet, blue, green and white (bone amber). Amber with a cloudy appearance due to internal bubbles is known as bastard amber. The blue and green forms also contain trapped air bubbles, which cause a fluorescent light colouration. Reddish amber is known as ruby amber. Some types of amber are also named after their place of origin, such as bacalite (Baja California, Mexico), burmite (Myanmar, formerly Burma) and roumanite (Romania), the most common being succinite, found in the Baltic, sometimes referred to as 'true amber'. Amber may be transparent or translucent and has a greasy shine and cloudy appearance. Over the centuries, philosophers and alchemists conjured up delightful but fanciful theories to explain the origins of this intriguing millions-of-years-old resin, with its trapped insects, pieces of moss, spider webs, feathers, eggs, reptiles, lichens and pine needles forever frozen in time. This honey-like crypt for all manner of prehistoric life forms, makes amber a peculiar material, and it is believed that it is unlikely to exist on any other planet but Earth. On a metaphysical and spiritual level, amber can be used to boost your energy and courage, to enhance powers of recall, and even to improve your finances. If you suffer from timidity and a fear of speaking your mind, it can instil bravery, inner strength and confidence. With its reputation of being effective at storing magical charge, it can be charged up and carried or worn as a talisman to attract more positive energy in areas such as love, success or luck. Also connected to the Sun due to its colouring, amber is often used in wealth spells; this may also be a legacy of ancient times when only the wealthy could afford to wear amber. Amber has uplifting energies, helps you to find humour and joy, alleviates stress, aids spiritual expansion and is especially beneficial for people suffering depression or suicidal thoughts, and helpful if you are feeling weighed down with responsibilities. Amber has a positive effect when you are feeling powerless or out of control, reminding you of your inner strength and past achievements. Worn as jewellery, it can be grounding and stabilising. When used on the Solar Plexus, with which it resonates, amber can enhance clarity about your future path or purpose. Amber quickly heals gaps, tears, holes and other wounds in the aura caused by emotional imbalances; it also provides protection against other people's negative emotions which may cause auric damage. It promotes trust, peacefulness and altruism, and brings wisdom. Overall, amber is a powerful healer and cleanser that absorbs negative energies and transmutes them into positive forces which stimulate the body and psyche to heal themselves. Still believed to bestow joy, spontaneity, purification of body, mind and spirit, confidence, and good luck, it seems that time has not diminished our belief in amber as a potent healer.

★ **CHRYSOCOLLA** ★ Chrysocolla comes mostly in striking shades of blue, green and turquoise, and is a tranquil, sustaining stone which helps meditation and communication. It resonates with the Throat and Heart chakras, encourages one to speak one's truth and enhances insight which help clarify one's spiritual purpose. It also connects and aligns us with Mother Earth, encouraging us to appreciate the balance of nature and to seek to attain this harmony within ourselves. Chrysocolla balances, calms, cleanses and energises all the chakras and aligns them with the Divine. It helps one to invoke great inner strength amid change or chaos, and is especially beneficial to flailing relationships. It dissolves guilt and helps to heal heartache, even increasing the capacity to love. Chrysocolla also enhances personal power, creativity, self-awareness, motivation and inspires confidence and inner balance. Overall, this attractive stone is said to promote and activate love, wisdom, peace, friendship, success, luck, protection and positivity.

POWER CRYSTALS FOR SECOND HALF SAGITTARIANS ★ (6 - 20 December)

Influenced by Jupiter and the Sun
Tourmaline, Turquoise, Hauyne, Bornite,
Chalcopyrite, Thunder Egg

★ **TOURMALINE** ★ Tourmaline in general cleanses, purifies, and transforms dense energy into a lighter vibration. Excellent for balancing and connecting the chakras, at a physical level this gem balances the meridians, and attracts inspiration, tolerance and compassion. Tourmaline is a potent mental healer and transmutes negative thought patterns into positive ones. As it is a high energy stone, it can boost vitality and uplift the spirits. The tourmaline's unique positive and negative electrical properties gave it its early name of the 'the mineral magnet' *; warmth also activates it, and it has long been associated with fire, electricity and magnetism. Coming in a wide variety of tints, no other family of gemstones has the richness in colour variation of the tourmaline, and within most tourmalines, rainbows abound. It is also regarded as the 'master physician' of the mineral world, with remarkable properties and a harlequin personality. Its myriad hues are the result of the contributions made by each single original crystal in this striking stone's composition. It is strongly protective, instils patience and teaches tact and diplomacy. It helps one to find the joy in situations, promotes inner security, alleviates depression and fear, and facilitates understanding of situations and expressing one's intentions clearly.

* In times past tourmaline was classed as a mineral magnet rather than as a gem. The reason for this was its unique electrical energies which cause it, when rubbed or heated, to produce in each of its crystals a positive charge at one end and a negative charge at the other. Tourmaline is pyroelectric, developing an electrical charge when heated (making it ideal for use in thermometers). For this reason, rather than encasing this gem in another metal, for example gold, it is better to use an open claw setting which allows the electrical properties of this mineral 'magician' to act without obstruction.

★ **TURQUOISE** ★ A very ancient and powerful stone, found mainly in Persia, where it is found in veins in rock, turquoise symbolises prosperity, strength and friendship. Magical attributes of this brilliant blue or green-blue stone are protection from the evil eye and dark forces, and attracting good fortune. Turquoise is regarded as a lucky stone, bringing protection and healing to the wearer. It is known as the 'horseman's stone' due to the belief that it protected riders from falls. This also explains its connection to the zodiac sign Sagittarius (the centaur). It is a purification stone, dispelling negative energy and clearing electromagnetic 'smog', providing protection against pollutants and toxins within the environment. Empathetic and balancing, turquoise balances and aligns all the chakras with the subtle bodies. It was revered by the ancient Egyptians, and favoured by the Native Americans as a travelling stone and to connect with the sky spirit Father Sky, to ask him to bring rain to increase crop yields and thereby increase prosperity. Indeed, without possession of a turquoise, no medicine man could command the honour, respect and veneration his position demanded; nor would the spear or arrow of the hunter fly true to its target. Turquoise is a symbol of generosity, sincerity and affection and it is believed to preserve friendships and make friends of enemies. Some superstitions around it are that it brings good luck on a Saturday, but to bring good luck, it should be given as a gift, not bought. An old Arabian spell for improving your fortunes which draws on the Jupiterian aspect of turquoise, is to place one of these gems close to a window at the time of a New Moon and gaze steadily on the stone and concentrate on your desire, then recite a simple statement of your wishes to the crystal, repeating it four times. Turquoise is a most efficient healer, providing physical and spiritual solace and wellbeing. As a protective amulet, it is believed to fade or change colour to warn of infidelity, danger or illness. Placed on the Third Eye, turquoise can promote spiritual attunement, communication with higher realms, and enhance intuition and meditation. Used on the Throat chakra, it releases old beliefs and inhibitions, allowing the soul to express itself once more. Turquoise instils inner calm while remaining alert, assists in creative problem-solving, and aids creative expression. Psychologically, turquoise is a strengthening stone and dissolves unhelpful attitudes, mood swings and self-sabotage. It even has the power to prevent panic attacks and aids recovery after a nervous breakdown. It is also said to stimulate romantic love, and has the power to manifest abundance in one's experience. Turquoise soothes the emotions and clears the way to enable you to go with the flow, to express and accept who you really are and to find your perfect life path with courage and fortitude. It encourages self-compassion and shields your aura from the negative influences or emotions of others, helping you to recognise any 'dramas' you may be caught up in that are blocking your progress or true individuality.

dawning intelligence of primitive man first visualised the meaning of numbers and associated it with spiritual significance. Numerology is the science of the exploration of this relationship in order to discover hidden meanings, forecast the future or interpret the character of a person. In its more modern applications, a series of figures which correspond to an individual's name and date of birth are calculated, and practitioners believe one's prospects, fortune and character can be deciphered from the results ^.

So what is numerology and how does one use it? Everything in the Universe has a vibrational frequency, an energy, a force, all vibrating at various rates, and we as humans are no exception, the difference between one person and another is their rate of vibration. This force or energy is constantly in motion and changing, and we can even 'tune into' and feel our vibrations if we are still for long enough.

Along with letters, sounds, colours, crystals, and many other things, it is believed that numbers also have vibrations, and when we are able to familiarise ourselves with our own numerical frequencies, we can use this familiarity to add power and magic to our lives. The numbers of our birth date, the letters of our names, and the numbers of our Sun sign and ruling planets, all have a unique vibrational frequency, and herein lies the key to understanding our self and our journey through life. Numerology refers to the knowledge contained within the numbers of our birth date and our name, and this is our own personal magic which can greatly assist us through life.

* Metaphysics is the study of those sciences that extend beyond the physical or tangible

HOW TO FIND YOUR NUMEROLOGY NUMBER

^ Your Sun sign's number was added up according to the principle of corresponding a number with a letter, for example 1=A, 2=B, 3=C and so on in sequence and up to 9=I, then beginning again at number 1 for the next letter J and following this same sequence. Following this system, the sum of the letters in Sagittarius vibrates to the number 9.

Your personal numerology number is determined by adding up all the numbers in your birth date until they reach a two-digit figure. The two resulting numbers are then added together again to form a single digit, which is your personal numerology number. For example, someone born on 3 February 1983, would add the digits 3 + 2 + 1 + 9 + 8 + 3 = 26 = (reduced to two digits) 8. So that person's personal numerology birth number is 8.

Each primary number or birth number from 1 to 9 has a specific meaning and is governed by a planetary force. The principle of numerology reduces all numbers down to the following: 1 to 9, and 10, 11, 13 and 22 *. The last four numbers only apply to people specially concerned with the occult and spiritualism - and can be studied at greater length through other sources if so desired - and can in any case be reduced further to a single digit if preferred. Your birth number contains a unique power, and therein lie your strengths, shortcomings and opportunities. It is beyond the scope of this book to outline your individual numerology number possibilities, so for the purposes of astrological applications, I have only included your Sun sign and ruling planet's special numbers.

* The numbers 10 and 13, and the master numbers 11 and 22, can be further reduced to one digit if so desired; however, they can be interpreted as they are without further reduction. The choice is personal.

BASIC MEANINGS & KEYWORDS

1 ★ Sun. Masculine influence, beginnings, independence, inventiveness, originality, leadership, exploration, innovation, ambition

2 ★ Moon. Feminine influence, cooperation, partnership, tact, diplomacy, harmony, unity, emotions, imagination, adaptability

3 ★ Jupiter. Communication, expression, youthfulness, self-confidence, creativity, inspiration, optimism, curiosity

4 ★ Uranus. Order, form, security, stability, patience, restriction, work, values, practicality

5 ★ Mercury. Freedom, inconsistency, change, variety, travel, activity, learned

6 ★ Venus. Love, home, family, sense of duty, responsibility, marriage, justice, nurturing, balance, gentleness, peace, friendship

7 ★ Neptune. Analysis, wisdom, mystical, spiritual, solitude, precision, research, integrity, mystery, psychic perceptions

8 ★ Saturn. Money, power, success, organisation, hard work, business, health, purpose, control, authority, mastery

9 ★ Mars. Completion, endings, Universal, service, humanity, philanthropy, loyalty

10 ★ Fortunate, creative, vibrant, stable, optimistic, original, successful, determined, individualistic

11 ★ Master number. Prophecies, inspiration, moral courage, missionary, long-suffering, foolhardiness, enlightenment, invention

13 ★ Misunderstood, fearful, changeable, interested in the occult, fatalistic, flexible, sacred, beguiling

22 ★ Master number. Powerful, successful, idealistic, attracted to the occult, creative, wise, successful, masterful, spiritually understanding

★ THE NUMBER 3 - FOR JUPITER ★

Names ★ Trinity, Triple, Trio, Ternary, Trivium

Arithmomantic connections with the letters of the alphabet ★ C, L and U

Ruled by Jupiter, 3 is a lucky number which enhances optimism, self-expression and sociability. Number 3 is a sociable, outgoing and friendly vibration. Associated with spring, and consequently beginnings, new ventures and fertile phases, 3 is the number of growth and expansion. Number 1 contains the idea, number 2 is the pair which comes together to carry it out, and number 3 bears the fruit. Three also signifies initial completion, the first stage being achieved. In numerology, odd numbers are viewed as stronger and more spiritual than even numbers, partly because, when divided by even numbers, they leave a remainder and are therefore indestructible. Three symbolises the creative process that begins after one becomes two and starts to culminate into 'ten thousand things' - the essence of creation. In most great spiritual traditions, 3 carries a special meaning. Symbolised by a triangle, it is linked to the symbols of the astrological elements and the colours mauve and amethyst. The number 3, to the Triad, was esteemed by many ancient philosophers as the perfect number. From an early age, the idea of 'three wishes' becomes a part of our mythology, it is a part of our collective lore that 'things happen in threes', and it is regarded as powerful and sacred as it represents the manifestation of life itself: number one is the potential seed; number 2 brings complementary opposites together (e.g. male and female); and number 3 completes a dynamic triangle, energy is created and everything begins to expand. It represents the three common stages we all encounter: birth, life and death; and the vessels through which we experience these: body, soul and spirit, or body, mind and spirit. There are three primary colours - red, blue and yellow - from which all other colours originate. The Pythagoreans believed in three worlds - the Inferior, the Superior and the Supreme - while followers of Socrates and Plato acknowledged three great principles - Matter, Idea and God. There are three dimensions of space - height, length and breadth; three stages of time - past, present and future; three states of matter - solid, liquid and gaseous; and three kingdoms of nature - animal, vegetable and mineral. Three is a magical number associated with the triple Goddess who moves through the experiences of maiden, mother and crone, and is linked to the Waxing, Full and Waning phases of the Moon.

Negative traits of 3 character types are procrastination, vanity, hypocrisy, superficiality, scattered-ness, impatience, carelessness and extravagance. You tend to be energetic, disciplined, talented, and likely to achieve great success in your chosen fields. In fact, you are rarely satisfied with less, as you are conscientious, proud and independent, and love to be in control. As a number 3, you may be bossy and impatient, but you have many good qualities. Fortitude and freedom are the keynotes of this number. Carrying the life-force of Jupiter, this is a number of creativity, friendship and extravagance. It is a perfect number for people who are or aspire to be writers, actors, entrepreneurs, or general show-offs. It also loves romance in all sorts of shapes and sizes, so lessons of prudence, trust and loyalty may need to be learnt. You are creative, pure and simple, but your needs for expansion and expression make you prone to do things to excess. You are generally happy, make a cheerful companion, and can adapt yourself to any kind of company. Your enthusiasm may incline you to be talkative, but your high spirits are so infectious that your exuberance is usually welcomed. A superficial 'show' may hide considerable spirituality, since 3 is the number of the Trinity. Number 3 people have good relationships with other 3s, and those born under 6 and 9. Number 3 is considered a masculine number, Jupiter is its planetary ruler, and Thursday is the luckiest day for Number 3 people.

Alchemy ★ Practically every religious or wisdom tradition has a trinity at its core. The three ingredients of alchemy are known as Salt, Mercury and Sulphur, or body, soul and spirit. With the operation of three forces, we have a living and dynamic situation. There are possibilities for change and growth. Two opposing forces can be reconciled by the third in a new and creative solution. Three encapsulates the essence and concept of a triangle.

LUCKY 'MAGIC HOURS' OR 'TIME UNITS'

One rule of magic, luck and power, as already outlined elsewhere in this book, can be found within the well-known phrase, "As above, so below." From the most ancient times, the planets were said to rule Earthly destinies and powers. Days of the week were named after the seven planets which were the only ones then known: Sun Day, Moon Day, Mars Day (French: Mardi), Mercury Day (French: Mercredi), Jove Day (French: Jeudi), Venus Day (French: Vendredi) and Saturn Day.

The planetary hours are based on an ancient astrological system, the Chaldean order of the planets. The Chaldean order indicates the relative orbital velocity of the planets, and from a heliocentric (helios = The Sun) perspective, this sequence also indicates the relative distance of the planets from the Sun (the Sun switching places with the Earth in this sequence), and the distance of the Moon from the Earth.

Before an action is taken in daily life, or a transaction undertaken, for instance, it is possible to choose the appropriate day and hour that will provide the greatest chances of success. By studying the planetary hours system, you will discover which actions are propitious to which of the seven planets or 'star-gods' and at what time it would be advisable to undertake them.

The planetary hours system uses this Chaldean order to divide time, and each planetary hour of the planetary day is ruled by a different planet. The order is repeated, starting with the slowest: Saturn - then, Jupiter, Mars, Sun, Venus, Mercury, Moon, then back to Saturn, Jupiter, Mars, etc., ad infinitum. The planet that rules the first hour of the day is also the ruler of that whole day and gives the day its name. So the first hour of Saturday is ruled by Saturn, the first hour of Sunday by the Sun, and so on. It is important, for the purposes of using specific planetary energies for our magic and wishes, to note that planetary hours are not considered the same length as our normal time-keeping slots of sixty minutes. Each day is split into time periods, day time and night time, beginning at around sunrise and sunset respectively. These two time periods are each divided into twelve equal-length hours, which are the planetary hours. So the planetary hours of the day and the planetary hours of the night will be of different lengths, except during the equinoxes when light and darkness are balanced.

In sequence, the Sun, Moon and the five visible planets each exerts its own special influence over a twenty-four-hour period. I like to call your planet's special day and hour the 'Magic Hour'.

Magic rituals to draw luck and love to you should be conducted at astrologically correct times and with the appropriate instruments, tools, cards, herbs, flowers, oils and plants which are linked with the ruling planet. For example, a love ritual, spell or potion demands a concoction of any or all of the above ruled by Venus. Do not underestimate rulerships, for they wield an unseen power that can help make our dreams, big and small, come true.

Further, as specific hours of each day are ruled by certain planets, if you are really serious about attracting some power, luck or magic into your life, it is imperative that you wish, pray or ask at the most opportune times for your Sun sign. There are two methods you can use for fine tuning your magical workings. The first method is to perform your spell, ritual or wishing on the day your Sun sign's ruling planet during the planetary hour that signifies the essence of what you are asking for (e.g. A Sagittarian who is looking for love might perform a love-seeking ritual on a Thursday, during a Venus-ruled planetary hour). Alternatively, if you wish to summon the power of your Sun sign's own ruling planet, then that same Sagittarian might perform their love-seeking ritual on a Friday (ruled by Venus) during Jupiter's planetary hour.

The nature of that which you are asking for, such as love, travel opportunities, money, career guidance, protection or friendship for example, should always be considered when choosing the day or hour during which your magic will be heightened.

The answer to the question why are there seven days in a week, is a very important one to know in unravelling the secret of your Magic Hours. Ancient people recognised the supreme importance of the seven heavenly spheres, which comprised those which could be seen by the naked eye: the Sun, Moon, Mercury, Venus, Mars, Jupiter and Saturn. They then named each of the seven days of the week after one of those spheres and assigned that planetary 'ruler' to one day of the week. As viewed from Earth, these seven spheres appear to move at varying speeds, and the ancients used this factor to arrange them in order of varying speed. If you intend to use your Magic Hours to attract wonderful things, you must memorise that sequence because it is what forms the basis of the whole system.

Whenever you intend to use your Magic Hours or, perhaps more accurately, Magic *Time Units*, it is important to find out the exact time of sunrise for the area in which you live, as sunrise marks the time when your planet's magic is at its most powerful on its specific day. So, at sunrise on Sunday, the Sun rules the hour following the sunrise, the Moon rules the first hour following sunrise on a Monday, and through the week the pattern is repeated, with each day's ruling planet beginning the cycle in that first hour after dawn. It is logical then, that the rest of the planets, in sequence, follow on with one planet per hour for that day thereafter for the rest of the 24-hour cycle, creating a Magic Hour or Time Unit for each planet throughout the day and night, depending on which planet rules that particular day and is therefore the first in line.

If you wish to explore the idea in more depth, it is worth noting first and foremost that each day contains twenty-four hours, but, depending on the season, day and night will be of varying lengths. In summer, daylight is longer than darkness, whereas the reverse applies in winter. During autumn and spring, day and night are usually about equal. Therefore, although a complete day always contains twenty-four hours, there are not always twelve hours between sunrise and sunset and another twelve hours between sundown and the following sunrise. So, depending on the season (and location), a time unit may be shorter than one hour, longer than one hour, or equal to one hour. So whenever you intend to use your Magic Time Units, it is important to find out the exact time of sunrise and sunset for the area in which you live. The next step is to divide the amount of day time (if day when you wish to work your 'magic', otherwise the same following theory applies to night time) into twelve equal sections by calculating the number of hours and minutes between sunrise and sunset and divide by twelve. An example is if the Sun rises at 6.27 a.m. and sets at 5.49 p.m., the amount of time contained in this day is eleven hours and twenty-two minutes. Convert this total into minutes (682) and then divide that figure by twelve (57). Therefore, each of the twelve daylight time units will be 57 minutes on that day.

Although this wonderful method of using astrology is very ancient, it may be completely new to you. You are in for a pleasant surprise though, because if you are willing to delve into a little research and put the system to the test, rich rewards are in store for you!

YOUR LUCKY DAY ★ THURSDAY

Basic Energy ★ Expansion
Basic Magic ★ Luck, Money, Increase
Element ★ Fire
Colours ★ Purple
Energy Keywords ★ Aspiration, Benevolence, Charity, Philanthropy, Generosity, Mercy, Dignity, Mind Travel, Expansion, Religion, Faith, Philosophy, Success, Understanding, Growth, Extravagance, Kindness, Humour, Optimism, Luck, Hope, Pomposity, Radiance, Reverence, Confidence, Indulgence, Opulence

Thursday is the day of Jupiter, your ruler. In commonly used calendars, Thursday is the fifth day of the week, though in others it is the fourth. The English name is derived from Middle English *Thuresday*, meaning 'Thor's Day'. In Latin the day was known as *Iovis Dies*, 'Jupiter's Day'. Thursday is known as this king of the gods' day. Thursday has its origins in the Saxon *Thor's Day*, and the Latin *Jove* (which links to the Jupiterian trait 'jovial'), from which the French *Jeudi*, Spanish *Jueves* and Italian *Giovedi* may derive from. In the folk rhyme 'Monday's Child', 'Thursday's child has far to go' - you can interpret this as you please, but I don't feel it fits with Jupiter's generally optimistic, expansive nature; however, it can be taken to mean that your horizons may well open up before you on your life's journey and you therefore have far horizons that await your exploration.

Jupiter rules over business and material growth, justice, the higher mind, legal matters, ethics, publishing, luck and general increase and expansion, so if you are taking action to expand anything in your world, or seeking judgement on or clarity about your affairs, Thursday would be a powerful day on which to ask. Thursday is a day of Luck, Abundance, Optimism, Expansion, Higher Learning, Hope, Positivity, Risk, Philosophy, Speculation, Adventure, Creativity and Faraway Journeys, and an opportune day for making wishes or working magic involving higher education or tertiary studies, growth, idealism, philosophical endeavours, influence, worldly power, accomplishment, wisdom, overall fulfilment, games of chance, abundance, optimism, and long-distance or foreign travel. Good luck, and always be careful what you wish for - because, as Ralph Waldo Emerson so eloquently noted, you will surely get it!

JUPITER'S MAGIC TIME UNITS
(BASED ON THE PLANETARY HOURS)
FOR EACH DAY OF THE WEEK

SATURDAY ★ Second and Ninth time units after sunrise
SUNDAY ★ Sixth time unit after sunrise
MONDAY ★ Third and Tenth time units after sunrise
TUESDAY ★ Seventh time unit after sunrise
WEDNESDAY ★ Fourth and Eleventh time units after sunrise
THURSDAY ★ First and Eighth time units after sunrise
FRIDAY ★ Fifth and Twelfth time units after sunrise **

Choose the Hour/s of Jupiter for any transaction, initiative or venture which is likely to involve an expansion, increase, good fortune, faith, celebration, spirituality, more comfort, greater possibilities in a situation, to arrive at a soiree or a party, or to choose or give a present or charitable gift.

** Please note that for the purposes of simplification, the information regarding 'Jupiter's Magic Time Units' is a very diluted and simplified version of using magical times to your advantage. These hours cover only daylight hours, or the first twelve hours after sunrise, and do not take into account magical times after sunset or throughout the night. 'Hours' is also a deceptive term, as most 'time periods' used in this system are less than an hour, but for the purposes of simplifying the technique, I refer to them as Magic Hours (to keep with the tradition of the term 'planetary hours') rather than magic 'time units', which is what they really are. Should you wish to do further research on your ruling planet's most powerful time units, or require further information about the planet/s from which you are seeking 'energy' from in order to assist your wish-making, other sources may provide you with more comprehensive and detailed information.

A LITTLE NEW MOON / MAGICAL TIME UNIT WISH RITUAL

Step 1 ~ Choose the Magical Hour and/or day that matches your intentions. The first dawn hour of Sunday, ruled by the Sun, is a great time for all-purpose magic, success, joy, abundance, prosperity, bliss, personal power & all-round expansion.

Step 2 ~ Write out a little wish list with the appropriate coloured pen on the colour paper which corresponds to your desire.

Step 3 ~ Choose a small stone of your choosing that is connected to your wish (or a number of stones, that are perhaps linked with your planetary ruler's number, for example 3 for Jupiter).

Step 4 ~ Find a nice patch of soil in your garden or any special place to you, dig into it, affirm your wish in your mind, place the crystal/s and piece of paper in the hole, then place a plant on top of the crystal/s and wish list.

Step 5 ~ Fill the soil back in over the roots of the plant and feed it with a little water out of a magical vessel (a small genie bottle would be ideal).

Step 6 ~ Thank the Earth, the Universe and the Sun (or whatever planet you are summoning the power from) for bringing forth your desires.

Step 7 ~ Repeat all day long: "Thank You, Thank You, Thank You!"

Step 8 ~ Watch your plant - and your wish - grow bigger and bigger as time goes on!

YOUR LUCKY CHARM/TALISMANS

The following are three 'materials' or talismanic symbols from which to make your lucky charms, and the planetary energy under which to do it, corresponding with your Sun sign:

SAGITTARIUS ★ Turquoise, Arrowhead, Tin, Jupiter

"When any star ascends fortunately, take a stone and herb that are under that star, make a ring of the metal that is congruous therewith, and in that fix the stone with the herb under it."
Henry Cornelius Agrippa, *On Occult Philosophy*

Charms, talismans and amulets are among the oldest forms of magic. A charm or talisman is a symbol, often used to communicate a thought, prayer or wish to, or to make a connection with the Divine. It is usually in the form of an object, which has been imbued with mysterious and magical powers. A charm may be as simple as a stone, a flower or a feather, or it might be a parchment bearing writing; the meaning and significance that you attribute to the symbol is what is important. It can be created by yourself (to best effect) or by someone else, and works as a tool to activate our subconscious mind.

You can use general charms such as a cross, or a universally lucky symbol such as a horseshoe, but you will exude and therefore attract more potency and protection if you make and wear the appropriate charms with the matching gemstone, set in the right metal and created under the corresponding planetary influence. While most people wear silver or gold, cheaper tin or copper may be more appropriate and indeed beneficial for your Sun sign. An amulet (for protection) or a talisman or charm (for luck), must also be made, ordered, designed or purchased on the appropriate day of the week for its power to be most effective. Your day, as previously described, is Thursday.

You can even go further and create or buy your amulet or charm at one of the hours and/or days when your planet is exerting its most powerful influence. It may sound complicated and requiring of forethought and effort, but if you are going to summon magic and are superstitious enough to truly *believe* that you can do this (and remember pure belief in something is the starting point of all manifestation), you should be scrupulous enough to do it properly. For your planet's day and time, please consult the information under the previous headings 'Your Lucky Day' and 'Jupiter's Magic Time Units'.

GODS, GODDESSES, ANIMAL TOTEMS & OTHER 'GUIDES'

Gods, goddesses and guides can be summoned to help you live your life to its optimal best. Some are connected with your Sun sign, while others may be of your own personal choosing, ones you may feel particularly drawn towards. Those which align with your ruling planet and your Sun sign, give a good indication of those who will shine a guiding light along your desired path, but you can choose your own too, based upon exploration, observations, research, meditation or simple intuition - I believe choosing your own, based on your inner *knowing* or guidance system, is a very powerful magical tool. However, to get you started, following are some animal spirit guide ideas for your contemplation. Good luck!

YOUR LUCKY ANIMALS & BIRDS

Horse, Lion, Unicorn, Eagle, Stag, Deer, All Hoofed and Hunted Animals, Elephant, Dolphin, Swan, Peacock, Bird of Paradise, Owl, Elk

"Somewhere beyond the walls of our awareness … the wilderness side, the hunter side, the seeking side of ourselves is waiting to return."
Laurens van der Post, *The Heart of the Hunter*

"(People) everywhere are being made acutely aware of the fact that something essentially to life and wellbeing is flickering very low in the human species and threatening to go out entirely. This 'something' has to do with such values as love, unselfishness, sincerity, loyalty to one's best friend, honesty, enthusiasm, humility, goodness, happiness … fun. Practically every animal has these assets in abundance and is eager to share them, given the opportunity and the encouragement."
Jay Allen Boone, *Kinship with All Life*

Some astrological systems, such as Shamanistic * or Native American Astrology, tell us that the Sun sign we were born under has a corresponding animal totem, which informs us about our characteristics and act as a kind of spiritual guide or mentor throughout our life's journey. These totems are described as Solar totems, because many of them share similarities with the Solar system and the sign the Sun was passing through at the time of our birth, and therefore relate to animals and animal behaviours which also correspond to environmental conditions and seasonal changes. These animals encompass many aspects of the Solar system, from seasonal relationships, to creature instincts, to reciprocal links with the planetary vibrations, and 'clans' within nature that you are inherently closely connected with through your date of birth.

Carl Jung, a master of dream analysis and interpretation, proposed that animals symbolise our natural instincts, operating through our dreams. He theorised that certain dream symbols, among them animals, represent core emotions and concepts, archetypes that will hold true for all of us the world over, regardless of so-called 'divisions' such as sex, customs, age or culture. In *Man and His Symbols*, Jung states that primitive societies believed that each person had a bush soul and a human soul. The bush soul incarnates as a tree or animal - a totem - and when the bush soul is harmed or injured, the human soul is considered injured as well.

Some of the most important and powerful spirit guides are those belonging to the animal kingdom. Both in ancient times and in some traditional modern tribal systems, people consult with animals for their wisdom and personal power. Even though most societies today have drifted away from this connection, it has never really left us, and different creatures continue to communicate with us on both the physical and spiritual planes in an attempt to speak to our souls and spirits.

As part of the teaching world, animals can bring us wisdom and survival skills, while others show us how to adapt, transcend or morph. Others still can remind us the importance of play and humour, and guide us around how to overcome life's challenges. Many are known for their loyalty and ability to love unconditionally and without judgement, while some have a grounded and healthy detachment, remaining true to themselves rather than pleasing others, an important lesson in itself. Whatever the qualities of the unique animal guides for your Sun sign, all have some enlightening soul-awakening traits that can teach us much about our own true inner selves. Ultimately, your animal spirit guides, and in particular your Solar totem animal, endow you with qualities that will enhance your life and help to activate your creativity, wisdom and intuition, helping to heal the broken or return the lost pieces of your soul and reconnect you to the natural world.

Your Solar totem animal (listed last on your lucky birds and animals list) is not the same as an animal spirit guide, which is based on metaphysical principles and is also based on your soul's mission in this embodiment - however, you can definitely make your birth Solar totem animal your spiritual guide if you wish, as you may find that its qualities, traits, symbolism and messages strongly reflect and define your own nature - or what you aspire to become, manifest or draw towards you. Your birth totem power animal comes from a place of trust and innocence, and represents the essence of your creative inner child. If you spend some time meditating on your Solar totem animal, asking what lessons it can teach, and reflect deeply on its character, life and habits, you may find it connects with you on a deep spiritual level and you can make the necessary changes to your life to draw in more magic and power.

Overall, if your life is stagnant or in need of healing or an energy boost, you can request your animal spirit or spirits to come and help you change your vibration, awaken your truth and arouse your inner forces. If you are aware of your animal spirit's presence in your life every day, you can use its particular energies to support, guide and teach you. And above all, pay attention to any signs and expressions of its lessons, and remember to thank your chosen animal guide for helping you.

* Shamanism is a traditional spiritual practice of the Native American culture. A shaman, one who practices this age-old art, is an intermediary between the human world and the world of the spirits. He inherits his magical powers at birth, but spends many years as an apprentice, so that he is usually much older in age before he is able to practice and call upon his skills. People ask for a shaman's help when there is a crisis on either a personal or wider spread scale, such as famine, drought, war or illness. The shaman makes contact with the spirits by going into a trance. First, he may perform a series of rituals, which usually include drumming, singing and chanting, and when these have brought on the right conditions, he leaves his body behind to travel to the other world. There he meets with the spirits of his ancestors, who inform him what must be done to relieve the suffering of his people. If the shaman is asked to cure someone of a dis-ease, then the spirits may accompany him to find the correct medicinal herbs or treatments for his patient.

YOUR FEATURE ANIMAL ★ ELK

The Elk's Message ★ Application of the spiritual to the physical self to bring about healing
Brings the totem gift of ★ Love, heartiness, independence, strength, agility, confidence
Shares the power energies of ★ Optimism, happiness, spiritual evolution, stamina
Brings forth and teaches the magic of ★ Understanding of human nature and Spirit, trust, focus

The Elk's power comes from the Earth and the 'Great Mystery'. Elk medicine helps us to know when our true soul mate appears. Regal and impressive, the Elk brings confidence when you are unsure or unaware of your gifts, and modesty and grace when you are. With the Elk as your power animal, you probably feel the need for companionship and group support. It teaches that you do not have to do everything by yourself, as help is always within reach if you just ask for it. Elks are indeed found in large herds and are rarely seen alone. They enjoy the company of their own kind, but also have a need for their own space. People with this totem animal need a sacred place to go now and again in order to restore and to keep their energy balanced.

The majestic Elk deserves and demands respect. It has a regal demeanour and a strong self-image. Having him as your totem animal means that you most probably often find yourself on life's centre stage, either in your personal or professional life. It is believed that generally, people with this power animal have connections with royalty in their past life/lives.

Part of the Elk's teachings is the art of survival. They don't graze at night, and if threatened by predators, the herd will scatter to the Four Winds to confuse the predators. If cornered, they can turn dangerous, the adult bulls possessing a full set of large antlers, which prove a match for any animal that tries to cross them, even bears. Elks can also be competitive, generally when vying for a mate, and will fight aggressively and draw blood, or worse. If you have Elk medicine and possess such aggressive tendencies, you must learn to practice control and fairness in all endeavours and battles you undertake. Even though these tendencies may not be apparent to your conscious mind, when you are provoked or threatened, they may surface unexpectedly.

The Elk's medicine includes strength, endurance, agility, nobility and sensual passion, teaching us how to make the best use of our energy and spirit. It also imparts wisdom on how to pace yourself as you work towards your goals - by learning this, although you may not always be the first to arrive at your destination, you will at least get there without being burnt out by the journey. Possessing admirable stamina, and with powerful and strong reflexes, Elk folk are able to run for long periods of time. Alert and ever able to sense danger, even that emanating from very subtle energies, you have high energy levels and well-developed perceptive skills. Temperamental and unpredictable, you can also be subdued one minute and irate the next.

The Elk teaches you to work on the way you conduct yourself, and to operate with power and pride, strength and empowerment. If you are lacking in confidence, call on the Elk to guide you towards becoming more impressive. After all, there are few more wondrous sights than a mature Elk, with its winter coat, standing tall, its antlers reaching towards the heavens, exuding an air of command and exquisite, powerful regality - and truly standing out from the herd.

SPIRITUAL KEEPER ★ BEAR

Your spiritual keeper guides your spiritual growth and brings illumination. Your spiritual keeper is determined by the season in which you were born. Regarded as the 'keepers' or 'caretakers' of the Universe, the four Directions or alignments were also referred to by the Native Americans as the Four Winds because their presence was *felt* rather than seen. The Direction to which your birth time belongs influences the nature of your inner senses. The West Direction's totem is the Bear. The Bear is a symbol of transformation, introspection, conservation, and strength drawn from within. The Bear has played a prominent role in many Native cultures, and because of its significance, a constellation, Ursus Major, was named for it. Bears can be amazingly fast and even climb trees, and many tribal people have regarded it as too powerful a medicine, fearing that the Bear would even hunt them and kill them if it was feeling threatened or starving. Despite its ferocity and the fear it can invoke, the Bear is considered to be a

Visualise the Thunderbird/Hawk in your spirit to be soaring high and being held aloft by the invisible hands of the Four Winds. Your eyes scan all before you and above you, and your keen perception is without equal. The Thunderbird's true desire is not to know what lies below; your true yearning is to join with Grandfather Sky. Fly high and keep your eyes focused ever upward.

THE OWL & SAGITTARIUS

★ Keywords ★
Wisdom, Knowledge, Help, Support, Revelation

The Owl is sometimes known as the Ancient Wisdom Keeper. The Owl has long been associated with the need to retreat from the world. Owl energy teaches us to look inside ourselves for the answers we seek. A powerful spirit guide when embarking upon meditation or study, the Owl will help you to keep secrets. The Owl is also linked with the night and Moon magic. This majestic bird is revered by other animals for its wisdom and knowledge and because it is mostly nocturnal and can see in the dark, is also linked with prophecy. The American Plains' Indians saw the Owl as a protector and ruler of the night, so wore Owl feathers in certain magical rituals to offer them protection. Athena, the goddess of wisdom, was given the Owl as her symbol and the bird has been associated with learning ever since. Owls can also be a symbol of evil or bad luck in some legends and cultures.

Though not all Owls are nocturnal, magically and mythologically they are creatures of the night. When they swoop, with wings outstretched and huge wide eyes, across the face of the Moon or pale against the darkness, they resemble ghosts, and indeed they are associated with spirits in numerous cultures.

The link between Owls and folklore is ancient. This bird was the symbol of ancient Athens, and the silver four-drachma coin bore the image of the Owl as a symbol of that city's patron, Athena, the Greek goddess of wisdom; hence the idea of Owls as messengers of wisdom. Athena's Roman counterpart Minerva also had the Owl as a symbol. In many other cultures, especially that of the Native North American, the Owl was a wise teacher of traditions. To the Celts the Owl and the Owl goddess were linked with the Moon. The Owl was the bird of the Crone, an association that was later transferred to banshees, especially in Scotland (a banshee might appear as an Owl flapping at the windows of the dying). This accords with the role of the Owl in warning of death, since an Owl heralded the deaths of the Roman emperors Julius Caesar, Commodus Aurelius, Agrippa and Augustus. Among the Maoris of New Zealand Owls are revered as guardian spirits of the community and wise ancestors. In the children's classic Winnie the Pooh, problems usually prompt Pooh to seek Owl for advice since, "If anyone knows anything about anything, it's Owl." It is the nocturnal habits of most Owl species that probably led to their being attributed with occult powers. This was highlighted by their noiseless flight, due to their velvety surface, their intense fixed gaze, and of course their superb night vision, the last which may be responsible for its connection with prophecy and its reputation for being all-seeing, clairaudient and clairvoyant.

Changeable, free, independent and as mutable as the wind, the Owl is a difficult one to pin down. With its easy going nature and radiating a natural warmth, the Owl is a friend to the world. Notorious for engaging in life with a tank full of enthusiasm, the Owl whole-heartedly loves adventure and challenge. Although he or she can be reckless, careless and thoughtless, he or she is also very adaptable and versatile, making a great teacher, artist or conversationalist. The Owl can be excessive, over-indulgent, extravagant, tactless and belligerent, but in a nurturing, supportive environment, he or she will be an engaging, enthusiastic and attentive listener. The Owl brings the totem gifts of a sense of adventure, wisdom, intuition, keen observation and discretion. It shares the power energies of silence, versatility, meditation, hidden knowledge, inspiring challenges, and putting one's heart and soul into everything. But perhaps most importantly, and what links it with Sagittarius, is that the Owl brings forth and teaches the magic of embracing all, optimism, night vision, oracle, clairaudience and expansion.

THE HORSE & SAGITTARIUS

Perhaps because of their key role in advancing and linking civilisations, horses have been regarded as lucky in almost every culture of the world. Charms and amulets in the shape of a horse, or a horse's head, are believed to help the wearer rise to new heights of happiness and achievement. And a horseshoe, a universally lucky symbol, is believed to bring good fortune and protection. Hanging one above a doorway, with the points facing upward, and the crescent shape of a horseshoe, make them even luckier, according to superstition. The horse itself brings the gifts of freedom, power and speed, its medicine helping you to travel safely on your life's journey, whether physical or spiritual, as well as reminding us of the importance to slow down and make time for those we love.

YOUR CORRESPONDING CHINESE ASTROLOGY ANIMAL

The Chinese Zodiac, known as Sheng Xiao (literally meaning 'birth likeness'), is based on a twelve-year cycle, each year in that cycle related to a particular animal. These animals are: Rat, Ox, Tiger, Rabbit, Dragon, Snake, Horse, Sheep, Monkey, Rooster, Dog and Pig. The selection and order of the animals that so influence people's lives, particularly in East Asian cultures, originated in the Han Dynasty (202 BC - 220 AD) and was based upon each animal's traits, characteristics, tendencies and living habits. Further, ancient people observed that there were twelve Full Moons in a year, and that, among other similarly related celestial observations, suggests its origins are also based on astronomical concepts.

The legend of the Chinese zodiac's story usually begins with the Jade Emperor, or Buddha (depending on who is telling the tale), summoning all the animals of the Universe for a race or a banquet. The twelve animals of the zodiac all appeared at the palace, and the order in which they arrived determined the order of the Chinese zodiac.

Each oriental animal corresponds with a Western astrology sign. For Sagittarius, it is the Rat.

"I am the self-proclaimed acquisitor.
I am a link yet I function as a complete unit.
I aim at encompassing heights
And strike my target
Sure and steady.
Life is one joyous journey for me.
Each new search must end with a new quest.
I am progress, exploration and insight.
I am the womb of activity.
I am the Rat."
Theodora Lau

Chinese name for the Rat ★ SHU
Ranking Order ★ First
Hours ruled by the Rat ★ 11 p.m. to 1 a.m.
Direction ★ Directly North
Season and principle month ★ Winter - December
Corresponds to the Western sign ★ Sagittarius

★ **RAT** ★ *Fixed Element Water*

★ **Keywords** ★
Charming, short-tempered, sociable, influential, verbose, studious, enterprising, successful

imaginative, generous, clever, industrious, critical, courageous

The Rat is the first sign of the Chinese horoscope. According to legend, Buddha summoned all of the animals in the world to his side. Only twelve animals came and the Rat got there first, and so he became the first creature of the first year in the astrological cycle of twelve years. Traditionally a yang animal, the Rat is a typically likeable, hardworking, ambitious and thrifty sign. People born under this sign influence others easily with their witty charm and powers of persuasion. Rats generally work hard to achieve their goals and are usually good at saving money. You have attractive and powerful qualities, possessing both the desire and the ability to achieve success and a level of prominence. The Rat is a mover and a pusher with leadership skills, and although devious and hungry for power over others, you know how to use charm, clever tactics and guile to attain what you want. You are willing to defend your loved ones at all costs.

YOUR METALS

Sagittarian power metals are Tin, Antimony & Brass.

Although the magic power of crystals is widely recognised and applied, the influence radiating from metals is often overlooked. Metal, too, emits a powerful energy and in fact, in Chinese philosophy, metal is considered so essential and powerful that it is classified as one of the elements, alongside Air, Fire, Earth and Water.

As already mentioned earlier in the book, throughout the writings of early philosophers and theorists, there are countless references to the unmistakable mystic connection between the seven known planets of the time, and Earthly affairs, ailments and objects. Seven metals were connected with the seven planets, to which seven colours and the seven 'transformations' were added. So the ancient alchemist came to share the astrological doctrine that each planet ruled a mineral: The Sun ruled gold, the Moon silver, Mars iron, Venus copper, Saturn lead, Jupiter tin, and Mercury quicksilver. Consequently, in alchemical symbolism the same sign came to represent the nominated metal and its corresponding planet.

TIN

Tin is planet Earth's 49th most abundant element and has two possible oxidation states. Tin is allied with your ruling planet Jupiter, because it is one of the so-called 'temperate metals', easy to forge and work with, which is a Jupiterian quality. Tin can be worn as a pendant, engraved with symbols, and is usually used for money attracting charms and for luck in general. A white-silvery, malleable, highly crystalline and ductile 'other metal' that is not easily oxidised in air, tin is a chemical element whose symbol is Sn. It is a main group metal in group 14 of the periodic table, sharing chemical similarity to both neighbouring group 14 elements (lead and germanium). The first alloy, used in large scale since 3000 BC, was bronze, an alloy of tin and copper. Pewter is another alloy, of 85 to 90 per cent tin with the remainder consisting of antimony, copper and lead. In modern times, tin is used in many alloys, one significant application being the corrosion-resistant tin-plating of steel. Due to its low toxicity, tin-plated metal is commonly used for food and beverage packaging as tin cans, which are made mostly from steel. Some alloys which contain tin to greater or lesser degrees, and which can be used as a substitute for pure tin to make Sagittarian talismans, are: Bronze, Pewter, and Brittanium.

PLANTS, HERBS, SPICES, TREES, SHRUBS, FLOWERS, SCENTS & INCENSE

Plants have long been associated with magic, medicinal properties, superstition, nutrition and even astrology. In ancient times, some were endowed with magical properties based upon beliefs of the time, but also upon anecdotal evidence that some herbal concoctions, flowers or essences helped alleviate and even cure uncomfortable, painful or dis-eased physical or mental states. Whether these were based upon 'old wives' tales' or beliefs in supernatural forces matters little, for in modern times we can prove and indeed *have* proven through scientific research and controlled experiments, that plants have their place in our health and medicine cabinets. Some 'magical' plants have aphrodisiac or narcotic properties, while others have formidable toxic effects, but all are considered in some way to affect the human system on physical, spiritual and psychological levels. Plants such as cocoa, tobacco and coffee, which have accompanied humans over the course of millennia, are still, more than ever, an integral part of our daily lives. They still incite the same pleasures, the same fascinations, and the same dangers, and some still carry the same taboos. It is interesting to note that more than 80 per cent of chemical medicines in existence today, and found in pharmacists' dispensaries, are made from plants.

In modern astrology herbs are often associated with the zodiac signs and have evolved from an old system where a specific planet rules each herb. The planet that governs a herb is chosen according to its appearance, scent and where it grows; herbs are additionally categorised as hot or cold, and dry or moist. In this way you can see how the nature of the herb corresponds to the nature of the planet. If you are familiar with your ruling planets' basic associations, you will find it easy to match it to herbs. Although you can simply buy whatever herbs you wish to use for your magic, the optimum effect will be obtained if you can gather them at a favourable astrological time. Once you are armed with astrological knowledge, you can choose a time when the planet that rules your chosen herb is in a position of strength. Keep in mind that each planet rules a substantial amount of plants, so if one isn't easily obtained, it should be simply to find another one to use for the same purpose.

There sometimes seems to be a wide variance in the list of herbs associated with a specific astrological influence. This is because the different parts of the plant have different rulerships and uses. For example, whichever planet rules it, a plant that bears fruit is naturally related to Jupiter, its flowers relate to Venus, seed or bark to Mercury, leaves to the Moon, wood to Mars, and roots to Saturn. So, as well as the planet that traditionally rules the plant, it can be regarded as having a secondary ruler according to the part of the plant being used. Although you don't need to work with a highly complex system of deciding which herb will suit your purposes, you can make your magical workings more powerful by paying attention to some of these nuances.

Essentially, different scents, herbs, flowers and plants have their own specific vibrations. Their essences should be worn on your skin (you can make up your own combinations using essential oils or flower waters), burned in an oil burner, inhaled from a cloth, diffused in a bath or bowl of steam, or burned as incense sticks. Many plants, herbs and spices, however used, contain gentle yet effective energies which will affect not only your wishing ceremonies, but also your moods, associations and emotions, which can assist in carrying your wonderful Self in the direction of your dreams. Lifted up on incense smoke, for example, your wish is carried out to the wider Universe. Try making your own, out of any or all of your power plants, woods, flowers, shrubs, trees or herbs!

Thirty-three magical, mythical plants are: Cocoa, rosemary, tobacco, thyme, wheat, coffee, sugar cane, cinnamon, hemp, tea, pumpkin, foxglove, incense, amanita (a mushroom), tarragon, pepper, rice, belladonna, reed, ginseng, clove, ginger, sage, maize, mistletoe, lily, mandrake, St John's Wort, poppy, peyote, cinchona, verbena and the vine *. How many of your Sagittarian 'lucky plants' (listed under the next sub-category, 'Your Lucky Plants, Herbs, Spices', etc.) can be found on this Magical 33 List?

YOUR LUCKY PLANTS, HERBS, SPICES, TREES, SHRUBS, FLOWERS, SCENTS, OILS & INCENSE

Cornflower ^, Chrysanthemum, Holly, Larkspur, Bur Reed, Cedar, Ash, Burdock, Feverfew, Mulberry,

Agrimony, Dandelion, Oak, Bilberry, Red Clover, Solomon's Seal, Mandrake, Clove, Hyacinth, Wild Yam, Vine, Lime, Birch, Sweet William, May Apple, Azalea, Chicory, Marigold, Sage, Carnation, Betony, Anemone, Samphire, Mallow, Goldenrod, Coriander, Horsetail, Narcissus, Crocus, Rock Rose, Hyssop, Basil, Angelica, Chestnut, Wallflower, Chervil, Aniseed, Cinnamon, Borage, Nutmeg, Mint, Jasmine, Thyme, Ginseng, Sesame, Ginger, Maple Syrup, Sugarcane. *

^ The Latin name for cornflower, *centaurea*, is derived from the mythic Centaur, the teacher of Achilles who, having hurt his foot, cured it with the juices of this flower. Cornflowers are known as 'love in abundance' and are used in love and fertility rituals, as well as in spells to attract abundance.

For Jupiter ★ Mint, Borage, Nutmeg, Balm, Birch. The plants associated with Jupiter are large and often contain an aspect that resembles a religious cross. Clove, Fig, Myrrh & Sage are connected with Jupiter
*

* Some plant products can be poisonous, toxic, hallucinogenic or even fatal if consumed. Always research first.

YOUR SPECIAL POWER FLOWERS

SAGITTARIUS IN GENERAL ★ Narcissus

OTHER BIRTH FLOWERS ★ Carnation, Sage, Dandelion, Wallflower & Thistle

NOVEMBER BORN ★ Chrysanthemum ★ Japan's national flower is considered a symbol of perfection of the human spirit. For thousands of years it has been the emblem of the emperor; warriors in Japan would wear this flower into battle to bring courage - and these emperor's men always won the war. In this country it is on the official seal of the imperial family; this is because its petals look like the rays of the Sun. The chrysanthemum is a universal symbol of autumn. In the East, it symbolises good fortune, happiness, longevity and wealth. In Feng Shui the chrysanthemum is one of the five beneficial flowers, representing joy and laughter. The chrysanthemum symbolises perfection which is often expressed as the well-balanced philosophies of life practised by those who call it their birth flowers.

DECEMBER BORN ★ Holly ★ Although it is one of the most enduring symbols of Christmas, holly was the gift of good luck among the Romans celebrating their midwinter festivals. The northern tribes of that great nation draped holly over doorways as shelter for friendly woodland spirits who would bring good fortune into their homes. It is believed that sprigs of holly in the house at Christmas time will bring favourable luck. Holly, emblematic of physical and spiritual renewal, also bestows the gifts of foresight, strength and resilience on those who are born in December.

YOUR FOODS

Sagittarius needs to feel they've travelled the world in their lunch hour, so if you're catering for one, be sure to shop for your ingredients at an international food store. Adventurous and foreign foods are best, and the tastier the better; boring, unadventurous, repetitive, bland or tedious is definitely not on the menu for the Archer. Locally-sourced food is all right, as long as it is flavoured or garnished with something outrageous, eye-catching and conversation-starting. Outdoorsy, active, adventurous and try-anything-once Sagittarian types particularly enjoy dense, sustaining pleasures of the flesh on their plate and their palate. Being naturally active, you often eat on the run, and being hot-blooded and considerably fiery, you would prefer a hot roast dinner over a cold salad any day. Bold, outgoing and a bit of a daredevil, you are likely to take up the challenge of eating exotic and out-there foods, such as Middle Eastern khash, offal, Scottish haggis, fried grasshoppers, Japanese wasp crackers, black pudding, tripe, escargot (snails), Dragon in the Flame of Desire (a.k.a. yaks' penis) and anything hot, spicy or otherwise extravagant; the noveler and fancy the dish, the more appealing you will find it! You love to entertain others but make a rather careless, clumsy chef, so you would better off hosting than cooking. Slow-cooked, dull, colourless or otherwise uninteresting, are definitely not part of the Archer's repertoire.

SAGITTARIUS POWER FOODS

"Let food be your medicine; let medicine be your food."
Hippocrates

Richly fragrant, sweet and scented foods, all ethnic cuisines, all gamey Jupiter meats (Venison, Pigeons, Antelope, Boar, Grouse, Quail and Pheasant), Asparagus, Chicory, Endive, Leeks, Turnips, Parsnips, Bilberries, Figs, Limes, Chestnuts, Olives, Currants, Sultanas, Tomatoes, Mulberries, Grapefruit, Rhubarb, Celery, Onions, Red Cabbage, Oats, White Fish, Dandelion Flowers, Garlic and all bulb vegetables are Sagittarian foods. Your power beverages are Dandelion Wine, Absinthe, Anisette Liqueur, and anything sparkling. *

* Caution: Always use essential oils, alcohol and/or herbs with caution and research each one prior to use, as not all are safe for use by certain people, or under certain conditions such as pregnancy, intoxication or illness. Some herbs and oils may be hallucinogenic, toxic in high doses, or produce other undesirable effects, and may be considered potentially harmful or hazardous if used or consumed before operating machinery, driving, or combined with alcohol or other drugs. Always consult a qualified practitioner or undertake thorough research from reliable sources before use or consumption of any of the listed essential oils, herbs or foods.

YOUR LUCKY WOOD ★ OAK
(Great to make a magic wand out of!)

Native Americans referred to trees as 'Standing People' because they stand firm, obtaining strength from their connection with the Earth. They therefore teach us the importance of being grounded, while at the same time listening to, and reaching towards, our higher aspirations. In Norse mythology, Yggdrasil, the tree of life, is a cosmic map that represents all life. The tree has its roots in the Underworld, is linked to the Earth through its trunk and its branches reach into the air of the Otherworld of spirit. The dryad, or tree's spirit, needs to be respected and asked when 'taking' from a tree for the purposes of magic. The essence of tree magic lies in understanding the qualities of each type. These can be drawn on for such things as healing and spell-casting. For example, the rowan tree grows high up the sides of mountains, often in hard-to-reach places, so if you need to develop tenacity or access to difficult spiritual spaces, you can call on this tree; the oak tree is durable and strong, so if you are needing fortification or firmness, you can gain power from this tree. When respected as living, breathing beings, trees can provide insights into the workings of Nature, cycles, and our own inner essence. Each birth time is associated with a particular kind of tree, the basic qualities of which complement the nature of those born during that time. Appreciate the beauty of your affinity tree and study its nature carefully, for it has a connection with your own nature and lessons to impart.

OAK ★ Oak wood corresponds to the element of Water and the planets Jupiter and Mars, and is a symbol of strength, sovereignty, courage, wisdom, wealth, honesty, toughness, endurance, rulership, nobility, generosity, justice, protection, bravery and power. With its towering height and wide girth, it also symbolises and bestows luck, vigour, love, potency, health and prosperity. The mighty oak tree has a wide trunk, very deep roots and deeply lobed leaves. The older a tree, the larger it will be and mature trees can be well over 1,000 years old (their life span is up to 2,000 years). Held sacred in ancient times, its noble attributes have long been harnessed for use in magic, and today the oak is still valued for its great strength and durability.

Oak is known as the 'King of Trees' and has a strong association with English woodlands, which has its origins in Britain's Pagan past. It is connected with the Summer Solstice; its wood being used to fuel the sacred Midsummer fires. It also has links with royalty and kingship: King Arthur's round table was fabled to have been created from a single cross section of a large oak. In the 'old days', front doors were usually made from oak; this was because, although the thickness of the wood helped to keep the warmth in and unsavoury guests out, its magical properties also provided strength, fertility and protection to the house or building. The word 'druid' originates from the Celtic word 'duir', meaning 'oak' or 'door'. It was believed that the oak was a portal to the spirit world and nature gods were worshipped in oak tree groves.

Acorn nuts, the divine fruit of the mighty oak, are said to increase fertility, sexual potency, longevity, 'immortality' and youthfulness, fostering virility partly through the sensuality of their creamy texture and smoky flavour, as well as the protein richness they offer. Both nut and cone have been used magically in fertility charms. Acorns are also omens of wealth, happiness and extremely good fortune. The acorn and the tree from which it comes, is a portent which signifies successful outcomes to any venture you want to undertake, and prosperity and growth in the future.

Furthermore, the oak tree's essence helps boost energy levels and to achieve our goals and manifest our desires. Oak is a grounding wood, offering the gifts of stability and strength; imbued with the tree's powerful properties, it can be used to make magical tools or charms. The power and durability of the oak tree are demonstrated by the fact its root system extends as far beneath the Earth as its branches stretch above it. Its strength is further symbolised by enduring what others around it cannot; it remains strong through challenges, and is regarded as being almost immortal, as is often attested by its long life and ability to survive fire, lightning strikes and other similar devastations. Oak is one of the most sacred trees, traditionally prized by the Celts and Druids, the tree's commanding presence signifying true alignment of purpose, balance and fortitude, and Witches often danced beneath the oak tree during ritual. Carrying any part of the oak tree draws good luck to you, but remember first to ask for permission and above all, to show recognition and gratitude for this wood's amazing gifts.

YOUR SACRED CELTIC CALENDAR TREE
★ ELDER

ELDER ★ (25 November - December 23)

The Celts and other ancient peoples had many beliefs and traditions based around the magical lore of trees. The system of Celtic tree astrology was developed out of a natural connection with the Druids' knowledge of Earth cycles and their reverence for the sacred knowledge they believed was held by trees. The Druids had a profound connection with trees and regarded them as vessels of infinite wisdom. Their calendar, being based on a Lunar year of thirteen months, contains a tree for each of these Lunar months, corresponding with (but not exactly) each of the twelve western astrology zodiac signs, which are based on the Solar calendar.

ELDER ★ The elder is considered a magical and holy tree by various cultures of western and northern Europe. Truly ancient, vestiges of its existence have been found at Stone Age sites. It was believed that elder could not be struck by lightning, and so was planted nearby houses for protection. If struck down, the resilient elder can grow from the smallest stump, and on battlefields it is among the first of the trees to spring back and return life to the destroyed land. The stems of the elder branches, their pith removed, were worn as magical amulets to protect the wearer from harm and also to bring health and good luck to the wearer.

Elder carries properties of exorcism, healing, purification and protection. Elderberries, blossoms or leaves hung over doorways of houses, are said to drive away spirits, serpents and burglars. One old magical chant hails elder as a bringer of prosperity: "Elder over the doorway, fortune over the threshold." But it can be used by the druids, or tree spirits, for both good *and* bad magic. As a sacred tree of the Celtic calendar, it can be used to bless and heal, but as ruler of the thirteenth tree month, the elder also has unlucky associations and, in the past, would have been used in dark magic to curse.

In Irish folklore, it is said that the sidhe- or elf-arrows were fashioned of elder and that the most potent witches' wand was one formed from an elder bough. Considered the tree of transformation, elder is the guardian of the thirteenth month of the Celtic tree calendar. This 'month' is three days long and contains both the end of the year (Halloween) and the beginning of the New Year (All Soul's Day). Celtic tree lore regards the elder as the tree of regeneration, representing 'death in life and life in death'. If it is allowed, this tree can imprint into your consciousness the sensation of harmony which arises from following one's inner prompting and experiencing the new life that rises out of death.

Elder types tend to be wild, free spirits. However, you may be misjudged as an outsider due to your tendency to be withdrawn in spite of your outwardly extroverted nature. Deeply thoughtful and with a philosophical leaning, you genuinely strive to be helpful to others, but your brutal honesty can sometimes trip you up and hinder any assistance offered.

ESPECIALLY FOR AUSTRALIANS
(OF ALL ZODIAC SIGNS)

If you live in Australia, here are two Australian-based magical woods, for those who prefer to source their woods closer to home and nature. Australia has a less documented history than many European civilisations, but still has no less mythology and legends swirling in its mists of time.

EUCALYPTUS ★ Eucalyptus is very plentiful and has a wonderfully intoxicating, distinctive, clean aroma which is reminiscent of the continent's vast areas of bushland, and has played an important ceremonial and medicinal role in the culture of Australian Aborigines, who have inhabited the nation for 40,000 to 50,000 years. Eucalyptus is a wood of feminine energy whose elemental association is Earth and main origin is Australia. One of the strongest healing woods known, eucalyptus wood has been used for centuries for medicinal as well as ritualistic purposes. Heady and Earthy, the energy of this wood is clean and pure. Eucalyptus is recommended for the promotion of good, robust health, and is also related to luck, especially if regarding knowledge. An excellent tool in divination, particularly when worn as a charm to invoke luck, it brings the wearer or user good fortune when used in rituals seeking positive results.

LEOPARDWOOD (or LACEWOOD) ★
Leopardwood or the Leopard Tree, so named because of its spotted wood, carries the energies of both the masculine and the feminine, Mars (Aries, Scorpio) and Venus (Taurus, Libra), and its main affinity is with the Water element (Cancer, Scorpio, Pisces). Leopardwood is a very useful tool for divination and is associated with positive luck, earning it the label 'gambler's wood'. Overall, its energy is very positive, making it an ideal wood for use in almost any ritual or spell, especially those concerning luck, magic and divination.

THE POWER OF LOVE

Each Sun sign exudes their own love and romance style. This style is an energy unique to that sign, and has the power to magnetise to that person their true, soulful match. Unhappy or unsuccessful relationships are often the result of incompatible Sun signs, personal values, goals, hopes, viewpoints or expectations. I believe everyone has a perfect soul partner (or three!) who is especially for them, and just knowing that special person or persons are out there can illuminate your life's romantic path. In this lifetime, we may not find that person or persons, but can still experience the joys and wonders of many other significant relationships which enrich and add tremendous meaning to our lives. Some partnerships are only fleeting, but the feelings they give us can last a lifetime, while others are more enduring, and the rewards they give us and lessons they teach us can last a lifetime too. Small gestures of love on a frequent basis, consistent nurturing and communication, and making the effort to understand each other, are just four ways to keep the fires of passion and romance burning long after the initially roaring fire has diminished into glowing embers.

Your whole natal chart would need to be examined to form an overall picture of your romantic nature, and although the Sun is a fantastic starting point, it is not the sole consideration. Regarding these other planets, in Carl Jung's studies on psychological astrology, and in traditional synastry (the comparing of two people's natal charts to determine overall compatibility), the harmonious link between the Sun in one person's chart and the Moon in the other's (usually the man's Sun and the woman's Moon) is considered the best indication for a happy and enduring relationship. More specifically, the sextile aspect, an angle of 60 degrees, appeared most frequently between the Sun of one and the Moon of the other in fulfilling relationships. Other positive planetary contacts, such as one person's Moon to another's Venus, or the Mars to the Moon (again, traditional indications of attraction and harmony) also occurred frequently.

The feminine personal planets in a male's chart (Moon and Venus), and the masculine personal planets in a female's chart (Sun and Mars) tell a lot about the inner self and how this is projected onto relationships. However helpful chart analysis is in telling a story about your relationship style and approach, it all depends not on your chart, but on what you do with the resources at your disposal, which your chart can indeed tell you a lot about. Relationships and marriages involving harmonious planetary and zodiacal energies between the two people tend to last longer because they are simply more 'flowing' and easier.

The signs in which the four personal and 'relationship' planets - the Sun, the Moon, Venus and Mars - are placed, coupled with the aspects they make with the other planets in the chart, give important clues into understanding the often unconscious drives within you that shape your relating style, tastes, mannerisms and patterns.

Expanding upon the other planetary considerations is beyond the scope of this book, but it is useful to know, particularly if you are interested in examining the dynamics of a current relationship a bit deeper, or are wishing to attract a new one into your life. But for now, your Sun sign is a wonderful place to start! Your Solar sign is regarded as being at the core of the complex - and very fun - study of relationships! So for now, we will begin this study of love with your essence, your core self, the brightest light shining from within - your Sun sign!

SOME LUCKY-IN-LOVE TIPS
GENERAL HINTS

★ To attract and retain love, the Heart chakra (an energy centre within the body) needs to be balanced and clear from blockages. The Heart chakra is located in the region of the physical heart. Its Sanskrit name is *anahata*, and its symbol is a twelve-petal green lotus flower whose centre contains a green circle and two intersecting triangles making up a six-pointed star representing balance (and also could be said to symbolise six as the number of Venus). Its element is Air and its colour is green. Balance in this chakra is expressed as unconditional love for ourselves and others. Crystals that can be used to cleanse and balance this chakra are mostly green and pink stones.

★ Pink candles (two, representing a couple, or six, representing Venus, is preferable) can be used in love spells.

★ Any 'love-attracting' wishing rituals should be done on a Friday (ruled by Venus) night around the time of the New Moon (signifying the principle of increase and growth).

★ Basil, otherwise known as witch's herb or St Joseph's wort, is said to be the most potent lover herb of all. Basil vibrates to the energy of Mars, which is all about lust and sexual energy, and it is used prolifically in all sorts of love potions and rituals throughout the world.

★ Ginger has a reputation as a potent sexual tonic and aphrodisiac *. Arousing and warm, it can increase sensual vitality, particularly in men. Being warming and spicy, its vibration aligns with Mars. Saffron is also regarded as a potent, albeit expensive, aphrodisiac!

★ Wear red and pink (associated with Mars and Venus respectively), as these colours in all their shades are said to incite passion, lust and romance. Green is also connected with the heart by virtue of its association with the Heart chakra and the planet Venus, and its links with fertility, nature, abundance of all kinds, and new growth.

★ Call upon some higher spiritual help. When working your 'love magic', some planetary influences, goddesses and gods that you can call upon are: Aphrodite, Venus and Eros/Cupid, and other lesser known deities such as Juno Lucina, Demeter, Freya, Ishtar, Circe and Hathor.

★ The planet Venus has developed a rich culture of gods and goddesses associated with her varying levels of love and passion. These include the virgin - Brighid; the fertile woman - Aphrodite, (the Greek goddess); and of course Venus (the Roman equivalent); the mother and provider - Demeter; and desirous or physical love - Eros/Cupid (Venus's son).

★ The pine tree is sacred to Adonis (Venus's lover) and is said to balance the male and female energies. Pine is cleansing and protective and, as an evergreen, symbolises life. Its cones represent fertility.

★ Cardamom is said to have aphrodisiac qualities

★ The three almost universally recognised symbols of love are the goddesses Venus and Aphrodite, and the Cupid. Venus is the patroness of flowers and vegetation, and represents the regenerative cycle of creation, as well as beauty, herbs and physical love. She can be called upon for general love wishes and rituals. The dove, roses, rings, copper, apples, rosemary and the ankh are some of her sacred symbols. Aphrodite is a Greek goddess who has the ability to brings lovers together. Her names mean 'of the sea' as she is believed to have been born of the foam of the ocean. She can be called upon in ceremonies and spells for affection, love, marriage and partnership. Some of her associated symbols are the Flower of Aphrodite, swans, dolphins, frankincense and myrrh. Cupid, the cherubic winged boy with a bow and arrow, is the Roman name, and Eros is the Greek name for the same deity. The son of Venus/Aphrodite, he is an aspect that represents lustful love and desire.

★ Heartsease, another name for the wild pansy, Latin viola tricolour, was one of the most popular additives to the love potions of the ancient Romans and Greeks.

★ In centuries past, when people were more in tune with nature and its cycles, ceremonies, rituals and festivals were held on certain dates or times of year. The following are some examples, and you can reawaken their powers through craft and ceremony: February 2 is Bridhid's Day, or Bride's Day, and represents the white goddess; February 14 is Valentine's Day, traditionally the greatest and most well-known love 'celebration' of the year; March 1 is one of the festival days of Juno Lucina, the light bearer and goddess of women and marriage; the month of April is especially linked to the love goddess Aphrodite; the Summer solstice which falls on or around June 21 is an important time for reconnecting with the spirit of love, fertility and marriage; August 1 is the first of three harvest festivals in the Celtic calendar: The Harvest Festival honours Demeter, the goddess of love, as bountiful mother and faithful wife; the Festival of Lights, Diwali, in October, is sacred to Lakshmi, the Hindu goddess of happiness, love, and good fortune; the Winter solstice which falls on or around December 21, marks the turning point from long dark nights to lengthening days, and is the time of the wheel of love when virgin goddesses gave birth to their children - it is also fittingly symbolised by evergreens such as pine, ivy and holly; in Mexico, December 31, the last night of the year, is traditionally 'wishing night' and is an opportune time to make a wish for a lover in the coming year, using evergreen branches to enhance your request.

* The term 'aphrodisiac' is derived from Aphrodite, the Greek goddess of love, beauty, lust and sensuality

★ GEMSTONES ★

When it comes to calling love into your life using crystals, the general rule is that any of the pink or green stones are closely aligned with matters of the heart and can therefore help you to entice the affections you seek. Although your Sun sign has its very own special gemstones, outlined elsewhere in the book, the following stones can be used by all the signs (except for the first point, which are your own sign's feature stones), as their energies and qualities contain the power to attract and create love in all its forms, from self-love to deeper soulful connections with another, or to increase states of being which open the heart, thus enhancing your abilities to magnetise love.

★ Topaz, Zircon and Turquoise ★ Using your Sagittarian luckiest crystals is a fabulous start to working on heightening your romantic zest, and making your sensual energy more potent. Yellow Sapphire and Amethyst are also useful in raising your attracting powers.

★ Rose Quartz is the ultimate love stone. It invites love into your life by helping to open your heart to receive love, and gently reminding you that you are worthy of love. Connected with the Heart chakra, it is the stone of unconditional love, enhancing all forms of it and opening up the heart. It is excellent for increasing self-worth and acceptance. The colour of rose quartz is pink, the colour of Venus, the amorous planet of desire and nurturance. Balancing and calming, it helps to heal emotional pain. Wear this stone, keep some beside your bed, or sleep with some under your pillow to remind you that love it coming your way - and that you whole*heart*edly deserve it!

★ Green Aventurine is considered the 'opportunity and luck stone'. Connected with the Heart chakra, it helps us to recognise opportunities and is said to place us exactly where we need to be for good things to transpire, as energetically it opens our mind and heart to increased perception to recognise lucky elements. It also promotes new growth, optimism, and is an overall attractor of good fortune, adventure and abundance.

★ Jade, on a spiritual level, has an affinity with the Heart chakra. It harmonises relationships, and encourages compassion and the establishment of strong bonds.

★ Emerald is reputedly a stone of constancy in love, and is said to have been brought to Earth from the planet Venus. Because it is green, it also holds deep associations with the Heart chakra.

★ Rhodochrosite can be used to attract one's soul mate. This stone, as with all the pink stones, can be used as an effective love magnet. It encourages you to appreciate yourself by teaching you that you are worthy of love, wholeness and happiness - and so opening you up to receive.

★ Malachite, Citrine, Rhodonite, Moonstone, Morganite, Beryl, Ruby, Mangano Calcite, Garnet, Red and Pink Tourmaline, Tugtupite, Rutilated Quartz, Lodestone, Peridot and Lapis Lazuli are also known for their love properties, and can be used or worn to invite romance into your life, or to bring and retain enduring love.

★ Clear Quartz can be used with any of these listed crystals to amplify their metaphysical properties.

★ Shells: Although shells are not technically a crystal, but rather a natural elemental material, they are associated with love and are sacred to Aphrodite, the Greek love goddess, and are often used in magic talismans to attract romance.

★ ESSENTIAL OILS ★

The following essential oils are known for their aphrodisiac or love-attracting properties also, and can be worn as perfumes on the skin, used in an oil burner or vaporiser, dispersed in a bath, used in spell-casting and wishing rituals, sprinkled on your pillow to imbue your dreams with inspired romantic notions, or in any other creative ways you can think of! **

★ Essential oils, flowers and herbs which contain natural pheromones or like substances, or increase pheromone levels in the body, are: Lavender, Frankincense, Jasmine, Nutmeg, Ylang Ylang, Sandalwood, Patchouli and Asian Agarwood (Oud).

★ The prime love oil, which holds Universal appeal, is rose. Reputedly excellent for both the mind and body, roses are the basis of more than 95 per cent of women's fragrances, and the petals have a long tradition of uplifting the spirits and soothing the soul. *Rosa damascena* is believed to be good for attracting love, while *R. centifolia*, the French rose oil base, is regarded as an aphrodisiac. Rose is traditionally accepted as the all-encompassing Universal fragrance of love, blessed with a reputation for opening up the hearts of all those who come under its spell.

★ Cedarwood oil has been used since ancient times in incense and perfumes. Its deep, woody scent helps to stimulate the Base chakra, increasing sexual passion and desire. Its sedative qualities aid relaxation and encourage openness. In herbal magic, it is also associated with spells for wealth and abundance.

★ Neroli, Geranium, Almond (as a base), Basil, Thyme, Vetiver, Gardenia, Vanilla, Rose Otto, Apple, Cardamom, Lotus, Orange, Ginger, Bergamot, Rosewood and Clary Sage are also exquisitely seductive and sensual, and can be used in any way you like to bring to you that which your heart desires. These oils, when mixed with your own pheromones and magical intentions, will naturally enhance your point of attraction!

** Always research first and use with caution.

SAGITTARIUS ★ LOVE STYLE

To Sagittarius love is open and friendly, a wild adventure to be relished and enjoyed. However ardent and enthusiastic you are, as a lover and in relationships, your freedom and independence need to be honoured and respected. But you are also willing to contribute much to the union, and provide the relationship with excitement, novelty, stimulation and refreshing honesty. The marked idealism that characterises the typical Sagittarian also flourishes in love. In matters of the heart, you are full of hope and hold great expectations. Fun-loving and sociable, you will probably fare best with a tolerant partner who gives you a large degree of space, and in return you will be a committed and passionate partner. If tolerance is not present from your lover, your non-committal, flighty side will run rampant and you will seek broader horizons. An incurable flirt and witty charmer, you win all types over with your noble spirit, gregarious nature and gift of the gab, so you will have no troubles attracting admirers, but if you are already in an exclusive relationship, this could cause some issues. Of all the zodiac signs, you are the most likely to have a wandering eye and an impulse to roam. In many ways a status of singleness, casual relationships or non-marriage suits you, as you like to be able to get out of something with a minimum of fuss if it no longer fits. You have a roving mind and a deep appreciation for big love, but your endless questing for meaning and future goals and possibilities can send your partner into a spin. Insecure, jealous clingy types or homebodies have almost zero chance with you, because of your love of travel and liberty.

Reliability is not one of your strong points. Your reckless streak may also give your partner grey hairs, so if in a relationship it is important that you curb any careless behaviour and exercise greater consideration and self-control. Never selfish on purpose, you do have a tendency to be clumsy with your words and actions, which can inadvertently hurt those you love most. All this sounds like you are a less than ideal lover, but the opposite is quite true. If your partner respects your needs and your wanderlust, you have the potential to be a warm, caring and amazing lover, albeit constantly driven by your need to pursue idealistic romantic fantasies. You are casual and light-hearted in most unions, as you are in every other department of life. You are rarely romantic, but do have a big heart and are unpossessive, allowing your beloved the same liberties that he or she allows you. You prefer not to commit yourself devotedly to one partner who might try to tie you down, for ultimately you are a free spirit who must move through life and its myriad experiences untrammelled and answerable to no one. If your union can withstand your many explorations, it can bear anything, and would be greatly enhanced if you allowed your lovers to share that ride across the galaxy with you. Heavy, intense or sensitive lovers also need not apply for your affections, as these drain your spirited energy and make you run for the nearest exit. And if you make it to the exit and out, we all know what happens to the Archer ... they will be gone, sometimes forever.

LUCKY IN LOVE? SAGITTARIUS ★ COMPATIBILITY

* Please note the following is based on your Sun sign alone. For a whole and integrated approach to relationship compatibility, your whole natal chart would need to be taken into consideration. Synastry (*syn*: acting or considered together, united; *astry*: pertaining to the stars) is a branch of astrology which delves into more complex areas, and is based upon the natal charts of the two people concerned, to determine overall compatibility, potential conflicts and suitability based upon celestial influences. For the purposes of length, the below information is simplified and only refers to Sun sign connections.

Sagittarius ★ Aries ♐ ♈

When two Fire signs unite, sparks can fly. Compatibility, excitement, passion and mental stimulation will keep this fire burning. Fire and Fire blend well together, but the Sagittarian need to seek broader horizons may make Aries feel insecure and not a priority in the Archer's busy life. After all, Aries needs to be first in everything, and a priority in *everyone's* life. The Archer's lack of commitment and regard for the Ram's sensitive ego can also be points of conflict. But for the most part, this relationship has dazzling potential. Stimulating, exciting, sincere and honest are the four best words to describe the Aries-Sagittarius partnership. Sagittarius encourages enthusiastic, active Aries who appreciates the Archer's optimistic outlook and frank honesty. Being so concerned with the self, Aries also reveres

Sagittarius's broader brand of vision and deeper philosophical nature, and will be riveted by the Archer's effortless charm and intelligent wit. Both of you will allow the other freedom, adventure and space to roam, as these are so intrinsically important to you equally. You may also take many trips together, as you share a love of novelty and new horizons. The Archer and the Ram are a naïve and idealistic duo, making the chances of success together likely. Overall, you both have the faith in the journey to make it work.

Overall compatibility rating ★ 9 out of 10
Lucky Romance Tip ★ To attract an Aries, wear the colours red or orange, and use the crystal diamond

Sagittarius ★ Taurus ♐ ♉

Totally different from the Archer in almost every regard, to the Sagittarius the Bull is either an interesting enigma or just 'too hard'. For the Archer's flighty spirit, Taurus might just be too cautious, slow, materialistic and dogmatic. Sagittarian Fire can make Taurus feel like the parched Earth, with all his ideas and plans. Yet the Archer makes the Bull giggle and teaches her to lighten up. However, even though the Archer may impart some great lessons to the Bull and vice versa, you are very different by nature. Taurus is one of the most stable, consistent, down-to-Earth signs who only feels safe and secure when life is settled and predictable. Taurus's strong desire to put down roots and possess her loved one, sometimes to the point of smothering them with affection, is at great odds with the Sagittarian need to feel free, independent and able to explore and wander at whim. Sagittarius is a Fire sign, enjoys change, seeks distant horizons and needs plenty of room to move around both mentally and physically. This will threaten the Bull's strong need for comfort, security and sameness. Taurus dwells on the material plane, while the Archer resides in the philosophical, intangible realms - another divisional point of difference between you two. While Sagittarius is broad-visioned and open-minded, Taurus lives in the physical senses and her perception on most areas of life will invariably begin and end with these. But the Taurean sensuality will intrigue and attract the amorous Sagittarius, and both of you have charm by the bucket-loads with which to win each other over. You are both loving of luxury and extravagance, but Taurus is more restrictive and practical, which could frustrate the far more liberal and fancy-free Archer, who spends money carelessly. Overall, temperaments are likely to clash in this pairing, but if the Bull can keep a tighter rein on her need to possess and the Archer can be content to cuddle up on the couch from time to time, this relationship could very well work.

Overall compatibility rating ★ 7 out of 10
Lucky Romance Tip ★ To attract a Taurus, wear the colours pink or green, and use the crystal rose quartz

Sagittarius ★ Gemini ♐ ♊

You and your opposite sign can laugh and chatter together for hours. Both cheeky, witty, lively and curious, Gemini incites the Archer to act on his dreams while Sagittarius respects the Gemini's restless, childish charm. Both Geminians and Sagittarians are footloose novelty-seekers, and in many ways you make a perfect match. Both of you are witty, gregarious and entertaining, and will share a lively and carefree existence. Opposite signs have a lot to teach each other and you both share a love of learning; however different your approaches are. You respect each other's opinions, yet Sagittarius can seem a bit vague and idealistic to the Gemini's more astute way of thinking. Air and Fire have a strong affinity, as do your ruling planets, Mercury and Jupiter. You will probably have a wonderful chemistry between you and make a strong impact on each other, but when the need arises, you both give each other the freedom you so desire. Both being independent and intellectual rather than deeply feeling, you share a need for adventure and busyness, and Gemini is self-sufficient enough to allow the Archer his much-needed independence. Stimulating conversation will not be lacking and you both love to share your sparkling ideas and mingling socially. The Archer has an uncanny ability to bring out the passionate side of the Twins, and Sagittarius's warm wit and charm will win the Gemini over in no time. You are both naturally friendly and gregarious, so are likely to attract and enjoy many resulting social pleasures and events together. If Gemini's superficiality doesn't clash with Sagittarius's broad-minded, far-sighted visions, you have the potential to stretch well into the future together.

Overall compatibility rating ★ 9 out of 10
Lucky Romance Tip ★ To attract a Gemini, wear the colours light blue or yellow, and use the crystal citrine

Sagittarius ★ Cancer * ♐ ♋

This is not an easy combination - the Crab is totally unlike the Archer in both personality and style. The Sagittarian may initially find the Crab mysterious and magnetic, but needs to beware of their tendency to cling or to hide, and their passive-aggressive tendencies. However, charming, chivalrous Sagittarius should have no troubles winning over the soft, tender heart of the impressionable and easily-swept-off-her-feet Crab. But although there may be an undeniable initial attraction between you, the relationship potential here is relatively low. The adventurous Archer is far too wayward and freedom-seeking to be domesticated by the home-loving Cancer. Cancer seeks security, while Sagittarius seeks freedom; Cancer loves staying home in comfort, while Sagittarius thrives on adventure and change; Cancer is private and hidden, while Sagittarius is sociable and extroverted; Cancer is clingy and co-dependent, while Sagittarius loathes being tied down or restricted in any way. Sagittarius's natural flirtatiousness will inevitably hurt the Crab's delicate feelings, and Cancer is often far too emotional for the much more mentally-oriented Archer. Security-seeking Cancer may not find her home in the Sagittarius's arms, as he is non-committal and flighty, ever in search of new, expanded horizons. The Archer will not tolerate the Crab's sulky moodiness, as he is an eternal optimist and has little time for reflection or brooding. You might give this partnership a good shot, as you both love affection and play, but an unbridgeable gulf may develop as you ultimately speak very different languages and exude vastly differing ways of expressing them. But at the very least you both have big hearts and the faith that love can indeed conquer all.

Overall compatibility rating ★ 6 out of 10
Lucky Romance Tip ★ To attract a Cancerian, wear the colours silver or white, and use the crystal moonstone

Sagittarius ★ Leo ♐ ♌

You two Fire signs have a natural empathy and an easy harmony. However, the competitive sparks between you can engulf you and leave both your prides and egos battered in the rubble of embers. However, two Fire signs can also spark wonderful discussions and mind games. You stimulate and understand each other, yet the Archer's restless spirit and elusive ways may leave the Lion cold. Independent Sagittarius may rebel if Leo tries to boss or control him, and the Lion's fragile pride might feel starved or neglected if Sagittarius is too eager for freedom and wider horizons. The Archer has little time for tantrums and theatrics, and the Lion finds the Archer's blunt indifference to romance a bit off-putting. Non-committal Sagittarius may upset the Leo's need for a more consistent brand of love, with the Archer's free spirit winning out over being tied down to anything or anyone. Still, Leo is impressed by the confident, active, self-confident and enthusiastic Sagittarian, and both of you enjoy extravagance, discussion and drama. You share a love of the social circuit, both being warm, friendly, open and welcoming to all and sundry, and unlike any other zodiacal matches, it doesn't seem to matter to the Lion if the Archer doesn't worship him. An outgoing and lively relationship, your rulers the Sun and Jupiter, exert a powerfully positive and optimistic influence over your union. Both generous and open-hearted, you will more than likely enrich each other and on the whole your similarities will override your differences. Overall, the Lion and the Centaur are both powerful beasts, so your animal passions could be stirred enough to evoke some pretty amazing sparks here.

Overall compatibility rating ★ 9 out of 10
Lucky Romance Tip ★ To attract a Leo, wear the colours gold or orange, and use the crystal ruby

Sagittarius ★ Virgo ♐ ♍

This is a challenging match, but one that may stimulate both your hungry intellects. Virgo's soothing reliability and cool sensuality can complement the Archer's restlessness - or simply make him want to take flight. At odds by nature, your Earth and Fire combination needs much mutual tolerance to work. The Archer's extravagance and idealistic impracticalities may bring out Virgo's worst, and his playfulness, devil-may-care attitudes, carelessness and flirtiness may also provoke Virgo's critical edge. Your needs may appear very different, but there is substantial potential for a good-natured rapport to develop between you. If anything, your bond could produce a very strong friendship - the Virgo's intellectual mind is highly appealing to the equally mentally-oriented Archer - and you will engage in countless discussions and analyses of anything, all of it, and everything in between. But cracks will soon appear in any romantic relationship you embark upon with each other, as Earthy Virgo is methodical, cautious, analytical and disciplined, whereas the Fiery Archer is impulsive, rash, independent and extravagant. Virgo is mentally equipped to concentrate on one thing at a time, deal with fine details and live in the present, while Sagittarius is wide-angled, hopeful and always looking to the future. Both of you are Mutable signs, which means you are adaptable and have a fondness for change, but these qualities will be expressed in vastly different ways. The tunnel-visioned, plodding, reserved Virgo may grate the broad-minded, far-sighted, optimistic Sagittarian, and the Sagittarian's adventurous, scattered and enthusiastic spirit may be dampened by the Virgo's staid, petty, pedantic, ordered and practical nature. Overall, there could be an initial meeting of the minds here, but it will become apparent over time that your differences outweigh your similarities and the divide could become too wide to conquer - even for Sagittarius.

Overall compatibility rating ★ 6 out of 10
Lucky Romance Tip ★ To attract a Virgo, wear the colours white or yellow, and use the crystal sapphire

Sagittarius ★ Libra ♐ ♎

Libra's Air should complement Sagittarius's Fire, bringing genuine enjoyment and hours of stimulating, delightful conversation. Libra's indecisiveness, however, may bring out the Archer's more tactless side. The candid comments of the Archer can either amuse Libra greatly or puncture his cool demeanour. Either way, the Sagittarian's optimism and mental agility have the potential to be a balm for the Libran soul and food for its mind. The two of you together are bound to make an effective united front in social situations as lots of light-hearted banter is a given. Airy Libra won't stifle the free-spirited Sagittarius with impossible demands, and in turn the Sagittarius will enjoy the enlightening, stimulating and delightful company of the charming Scales. Both enjoy their freedom and independence in their own ways, and Fire complements Air perfectly in this blend. The union of your ruling planets Venus and Jupiter increases the qualities of love, happiness, success, abundance, pleasure and the overall ability to enjoy life. Although Libra needs to share things with someone exclusive and the Archer is rather non-committal, the Scales will allow for this because his Airy nature endows him with a healthy level of detachment and tolerance. Sagittarius in turn is generous enough to allow Libra to indulge in those much-loved pleasures, indulgences, luxuries and the 'good life', which he will revel in also. In living the high life however, and with their combined extravagant and indulgent tastes, these two could find their budgets - and their waistlines - stretched considerably! But aside from some minor differences, the Archer's spiritual ideals inspire Libra and the Scales can only benefit from Sagittarius's optimism, energy and buoyancy. Your energies flow together easily so long-term success is likely.

Overall compatibility rating ★ 9 out of 10
Lucky Romance Tip ★ To attract a Libran, wear the colours pink and blue, and use the crystal opal

Sagittarius ★ Scorpio * ♐ ♏

This is a dangerous and unpredictable liaison as the Sagittarius is sure to get something he hadn't expected with the Scorpion. In essence, the Archer should watch his tactlessness or it will be revenged. The Scorpio may prove too powerful and intense for the Sagittarius's light-hearted and freedom-seeking nature. The open, direct manner of the Archer can be charming at first, but a big problem if the Archer reveals the Scorpio's deepest secrets to all and sundry, as he is prone to do. Sagittarius needs freedom; the Scorpion needs security. The Sagittarius may become agitated if the Scorpio tries to possess or control him, and the Scorpio will feel slighted by Sagittarius's natural tendency to be insensitive and indifferent to feelings. Scorpio likes to keep her cards close to her chest, while Sagittarius has a need to know everything about everyone and lays it all out stark and bare. With the Archer, what you see is what you get, which is a far cry from the very hidden, inner-dwelling Scorpio. Generally, the Sagittarius's need to be free and explore the world at large will arouse the suspicions of the deeply mistrustful Scorpion, who will wallow and brood - something the Archer will not tolerate. Scorpio demands much of herself and others, but Sagittarius is a natural born rebel who will revolt against any attempts by anyone to pin him down, restrict his movements or question his whereabouts. However, the Archer's natural exuberance, optimism and enthusiasm can be refreshing for the harping, sceptical Scorpio, but it could have the entirely opposite effect also - Sagittarius natural openness and frankness could either fascinate, intrigue, mystify or enrage the Scorpio. The Archer does not hold grudges, and fails to understand why the Scorpion would feel offended by his flirting and wide and varied social circle, which is open all hours and where everyone is welcome. Sagittarius will also feel unsettled by Scorpio's deep, dark complexities and Scorpio will not understand why Sagittarius can just skip off in the other direction whistling a happy-go-lucky tune like nothing has happened. Overall, this could be a passionate match, but could just as likely frustrate both parties as you are both so different in expression and style.

Overall compatibility rating ★ 7 out of 10

Lucky Romance Tip ★ To attract a Scorpio, wear the colours red or burgundy, and use the crystal malachite

Sagittarius ★ Sagittarius ♐ ♐

Two Archers together can happily shoot arrows towards their dreams and desires - and hit the mark every time. Be careful of burnout from too much indulgent, careless play though! This is good friendship material and carries a great potential for the meeting of two magical minds. Both idealistic to a fault, you may build your relationship based on these ideals and fail to see when or where it is not working. This, combined with the fact that you are both so often off enjoying your own separate adventures, needs to be allowed for if your partnership is to work. Certainly, you both respect each other's need for space, freedom and independence, but this can create a situation where you give each other almost too lengthy a leash and one or both of you is prone to wander off. You are both likely to be reckless and extravagant, but this won't be too much of a problem unless one of you is in charge of the budget. Generally, this Fiery combination in two such optimistic, happy-go-lucky and jubilant characters is sure to create a big, raging bonfire. Fun will never be in short supply, and monotony will never be a feature. Overall, two wild, free and adventurous Centaurs galloping off into the distant horizons together are certain to share a grand and memorable love affair. There is a high chance that you will understand each other splendidly and be enraptured by each other completely. It is just important to be in the same country occasionally, so you can actually share the joys together *in person*.

Overall compatibility rating ★ 9 out of 10
Lucky Romance Tip ★ To attract another Sagittarius, wear the colour deep purple or royal blue, and use the crystal zircon.

Sagittarius ★ Capricorn ♐ ♑

With the Archer's clownish and wandering ways, he can either bring out the Goat's gallantry or stern disapproval. If the Sagittarian restless spirit begins to take flight, Capricorn will turn cold. The Goat's practicality and hard-nosed realism can suffocate the Archer's Fire. Sagittarius's bubbly mirth and innate goodwill may begin to lessen under the influence of the tough, rigid Capricorn. Pragmatic Capricorn will look closely and critically at Sagittarius's never-ending ideals, plans and bigger picture schemes, which will frustrate the liberal Archer and make him feel sober and stifled. Yet, more than any of the other signs, Capricorn can help to ground the lofty Sagittarian ideals and bring them to tangible fruition, which the Archer will greatly appreciate. But the differences between you may weigh your union down over time, as the marked contrast between Fire and Earth is so very evident here. While Capricorn is dutiful, responsible, cautious, serious, prudent, cynical and conservative, the Sagittarius is naturally hopeful, optimistic, buoyant, careless and impulsive. The Sagittarius's tendency to be extravagant and not care about consequences may be unnerving to the much more calculated, methodical Capricorn. Furthermore, your ruling plants bring another restrictive influence to this partnership, as Saturn relates to contraction, boundaries, limitation and restriction, while Jupiter epitomises expansion, abundance, boundlessness and increase. Although opposites *can* attract, the vast differences inherent in your characters may make your relationship seem like hard slog at times. But you both aim high, so your ambitious streaks could combine to reach great heights and achieve wonderfully special things.

Overall compatibility rating ★ 5.5 out of 10
Lucky Romance Tip ★ To attract a Capricorn, wear the colours brown or black, and use the crystal garnet

Sagittarius ★ Aquarius ♐ ♒

Air and Fire have a strong affinity, as do your ruling planets Uranus, the lord of lightning, and Jupiter, the god of thunder. Water Bearers like to speak their minds and express their opinions as much as the Archer does, and you are both idealistic and overall very well-matched. As you both value idealism and freedom, this could make for an unpredictable, zany and unforgettable ride! These two will have a wonderful chemistry between them and make a strong impact on each other, but when the need arises, they both give each other the freedom they so desire. Both being independent and intellectual rather than deeply feeling, you share incredibly idealistic natures that usually remain as pie-in-the-sky notions, but which thrill you nonetheless, and can provide endless fodder for stimulating conversation. Indeed, you both love to share your sparkling ideals which transcend the personal, mundane level. The Archer has an uncanny ability to bring out the passionate side of the Water Bearer, and you are the most likely of all the combinations to be sexually compatible. Sagittarius's warm wit and charm will win over Aquarius's cool nature, and Aquarius's aloof glamour will appeal to the Sagittarian's accepting and embracing heart. You are both naturally friendly and gregarious, so are likely to attract and enjoy many resulting social pleasures and events together. Aquarius's eccentricities, quirks and unpredictability may perplex the more open-hearted Sagittarius, but will nonetheless provide an endless source of intrigue, delight and bedazzlement.

Overall compatibility rating ★ 9 out of 10
Lucky Romance Tip ★ To attract an Aquarian, wear the colours electric blue or turquoise, and use the crystal aquamarine

Sagittarius ★ Pisces * ♐ ♓

While Water and Fire generally don't share a strong affinity, you seem to share many similarities as well as a ruling planet, Jupiter (albeit a secondary ruler of Pisces, since the discovery of Neptune). Both ruled by the expansive and optimistic Jupiter, you dream big and love large. Sagittarius loves to listen to Pisces' whimsical fantasies, but her tales of woe and sensitivities may set the Archer firing - either arrows of desire or derision. You are both idealistic, giving, generous and helpful, and have a mutual appreciation of religion, Universality, philosophy, philanthropical interests, charitable causes, travel, and humanitarian and other lofty ideals. Jupiter, the god of thunder, combines well with Watery Neptune, but this combination of energies can just as easily create waves and turbulence. This pairing is full of complexities and although it presents a multitude of possibilities in some types of human relationships, such as marriage, friendship and family, it can also can present issues around confusion, uncertainty or wishful thinking. Both being idealistic, many ideas may never make it past the talking phase, which you two love to do - share thoughts and ideas. Pisces and Sagittarius are likely to have a wonderful chemistry between them and make a strong impact on each other, and when the need arises, they both give each other the freedom they so desire. But while the Archer is head-based, the Fish is heart-based, and the Archer may feel stifled by Pisces's oversensitive, dreamy, and deeply emotional nature. Further, direct and frank Sagittarius may feel impatient with the Piscean tendency to be indecisive, vague and weak-willed. Sagittarius is rarely sentimental, and although spirited, chivalrous and charming, it is all one big fun adventure and the Piscean can feel hurt by the Archer's bluntness, nonchalance and apparent indifferent attitude towards their relationship at times. The Fish will easily fall hook, line and sinker for the warm Sagittarius heart, but her vivid imagination will conjure up the worse possible scenario when Sagittarius feels the need to break free for a little while. Overall, if Sagittarius can tolerate Pisces's tendency to be disorganised and scatterbrained, and if Pisces can accept Sagittarius's ongoing need for independence and far-reaching horizons, these two can make it work - and may even explore those glistening greener pastures *together*.

Overall compatibility rating ★ 7.5 out of 10
Lucky Romance Tip ★ To attract a Pisces, wear the colours mauve or sea green, and use the crystal amethyst

* With all Fire and Water combinations (i.e. Sagittarius with Cancer, Scorpio or Pisces), it is easy to see how and why fire and water are natural enemies. Water can quickly put a fire out, and fire can dry up water. Fire usually works quickly, and water gently. In alchemy and astrology, both are important, and both must be carefully manipulated and controlled to make full effective use of their powerful, albeit vastly differing, natures. Fire can be brought back to a steady heat, whereas the pressure and force of water can be increased vigorously or to circulate more actively. As warm and watery beings, the human body demonstrates the miracle of fire and water combined. Water connects, flows and lubricates, and brings healing, its passive, gentle nature soothing away the scorching harshness of fire. One ancient text offers a mystical view of how water and fire are intertwined in the body, and suggests that it is through consciously combining these two elements that we can transform our inner state. Fire can initiate and inspire this quest for self-transformation, but once the fire burns down, life can be restored anew by water. Natural enemies? Mostly. Astrological passion? Absolutely!

YOUR TAROT CARDS ★ FOR LUCK, MAGIC, ENERGY, ABUNDANCE, QUESTING & MEANING
TEMPERANCE, WHEEL OF FORTUNE & JUDGEMENT

Tarot and astrology are inextricably linked. All the cards of the Major Arcana, which comprises 22 of the Tarot's 78 cards, are 'ruled by' or connected with either one of the twelve zodiac signs, the planets and luminaries, or one of the four elements.

The 22 Major Arcana cards contain the richest symbolism of all the cards in the Tarot deck, each carrying a myriad of messages for the reader to decipher. The symbolism contained within these images represents the archetypal aspects of your character. It also describes the path your soul takes through each stage of life, revealing clues through which you can explore different parts of yourself. Each of the cards also represents an aspect of Universal human experience and has a name that either directly conveys the meaning of the card, such as Strength or Justice, or depicts individuals that represent these human archetypes, such as the Hermit or the Empress. The illustrations on each card contain one or more figures and tuning into a card's imagery enables you to grasp its meaning intuitively. Consider the demeanour of the characters, whether it is day or night, the background, any symbols, the buildings, the colours, the vegetation, the weather and the season. Every card has its own story to impart, and through entering that story you can gain deeper insights into the full picture of your journey so far, as well as illuminating your path ahead.

I have outlined three cards here for your sign: Temperance, Wheel of Fortune and Judgement, all of which have links to your zodiac sign itself Sagittarius, your ruling planet Jupiter, and your element of Fire. All three cards will have special meaning for your sign, and can carry powerful messages and lessons for you to reflect upon.

★ TEMPERANCE ★
Ruled by Sagittarius

Keywords ★ Moderation, Balance, Blending

★ KEY THEMES ★
Moderation ★ Successful Blend ★ Balance ★ Union of Opposites ★ Successful Partnerships ★ Blended Ideas ★ Pleasant Relationships ★ Cooperation ★ Revelation ★ Self-restraint ★ Waiting for Perfect Timing ★ Message ★ Regeneration ★ Advantageous Transactions and Negotiations ★ Mutual Understanding ★ Opportunities

Number ★ 14
Astrological Signs ★ Cancer & Sagittarius

With transformation comes the lessons of moderation and perspective. Temperance is all about tolerating differences, learning patience and waiting rather than rushing in head-first.

THE MESSAGE ★ In Tarot tradition, the Temperance card represents the empowerment of Alchemy, that mystical process of blending the parts of the self until fusion is achieved and the 'philosopher's stone' is created. However, we use our personal magic, there are times in everyone's life when things work out well and when everything runs smoothly. Temperance suggests that such a time is on its way to you, perhaps after a considerable period of inner conflict. This card shows a young woman pouring liquid from one container to another, suggesting the mixture of ingredients to formulate just the right potion. The success of the experiment will depend not only upon how well the various ingredients of circumstance are blended but on the attention and patience shown to ensure that everything is mixed at the right time. Temperance is all about balance and moderation. It also signifies cooperation and compromise, keeping a moderate pace and striking equilibrium between contemplation and action. This card is also about working in concert with others, and encourages you to see things from their points of view and to work in unison with them. Extending this compassion, kindness and tolerance are key to manifesting your dreams. Forgiveness will also allow for healing, which will help bring about the new beginnings you so desire.

THE STORY ★ Temperance is one of the three virtues to appear in the Tarot - the other two are Justice and Strength. Temperance reveals the ability to maintain equilibrium even in the middle of chaotic change. The freedom to discover new aspects of yourself leads you to explore your inner space once more. You become aware that if you are balanced and centred, life flows more smoothly. Enthralling you with the sense of harmony this creates, you discover qualities that can be explored from the inside then expressed outwardly. When this card appears in a reading, it means you are in fine balance, or about to become so. The natural movements of energy around and within you are in harmony and integrated; you are not fragmented or disconnected from yourself. You may even feel in a heightened state of consciousness, able to absorb much more than usual and to assimilate it naturally within your being. You may be experiencing a new sense of courage and wellbeing. This card carries with it an enormous power. If it is a gift managed with clarity and love, its message has been received. Feel free to use your powers wisely.

THE AWAKENING ★ An angel is featured on the Temperance card. This is the ancient depiction of a messenger. But she is not just a simple conveyor of a message; she advises and moderates while he passes on the information. Without the circulation of information and the transmission of energetic currents, no life would be possible. In the same way as water - which, because it follows the rotational movement of the Earth, flows ceaselessly and continuously, fertilising and regenerating the Earth - so flow the currents of life and of thoughts. They circulate within and through us, renewing themselves as well as us. These energies are like a source of nourishment, and this nourishing cord is pictured on the Temperance card, as the continuous flow of water being decanted between the two vessels by the angel. They ultimately stand for fruitfulness, action, flow, life and vitality, but always tempered with wisdom and restraint.

Temperance is all about the process of refining something to make it more balanced and thereby making it work more effectively. A good example of the concept of the word temperate is the temperate zone on Earth, which is situated between the frozen wastes of the poles and the burning heat of the equator. It takes from both these areas and moderates the temperature and conditions between the two, making a part of the world where people can live more comfortably and plant and animal life can flourish.

The dialogue is always open with Temperance, its presence reassuring because it tells you simply that, with time, everything becomes transformed and ultimately sorted out. Of course, it also pledges moderation, understanding, and tolerance, and finally, by allowing this free flow of energies and currents, it presents you with new opportunities and possibilities which you may seize.

SYMBOLISM *★ Temperance is a symbol for moderation and balance, indicating the need for an attitude of staying centred and avoiding extremes. The angel depicted on the card is representative of the spiritual aspect of ourselves. She rests her feet on both the land and the water, symbolising the harmony of the physical body and the emotions, and the grounding of ideas received from the waters of the subconscious so that they may be put to practical use.

Most cards depict a winged angelic figure who is pouring liquid from one container into another, representing the flow of the unseen and mysterious into the seen and known, or from the unconscious mind to the conscious, showing the need for the constant flow between the two. It is also said to symbolise the past merging with the future.

Some decks show the cups as gold and silver, symbolising the conscious and the unconscious mind and the need for movement between them. She represents the balance between the conscious and the unconscious mind, and echoes the teachings of the ancient Greek oracle at Delphi, which advocated "moderation in all things," as well as the doctrines of the Buddha, which encourage us to always seek the middle way over and above extremes.

Water flows back and forth between the two cups, symbolising the combining of energies to create a union of opposites. The cups represent our ability to receive and exchange information.

The pool shown in the picture represents the subconscious, from which flows ideas, dreams, inspiration and creativity. The water is moving, showing that the energy is mobile but always accessible.

The word 'temperance' means moderation and a lack of extremes. It is one of the cardinal virtues. The angel of Temperance strives for a sense of emotional calm and serenity, and offers the qualities of compassion and forgiveness.

This card relates to mixture and combination. Its meaning is to exercise careful control of volatile factors so that they result in a successful conclusion. Temperance is a card of healing and harmony indicated by the figure pouring water from one vessel to another, thereby encouraging us to let our life force flow freely. It counsels us that compromise is the answer to any problem and suggests the need for cooperation. It is now time to work with others in a collaborative way, sharing and pooling resources rather than hoarding them. It denotes a time to seeks others to support your endeavours and find ways of working as a team rather than in opposition. After all, prosperous relationships are those in which both parties work together keeping the other's best interests at heart for the good of the whole. The liquid being poured from one vessel to the other also suggests that relationships are positively enhanced by the sharing of feelings, for after all, if water doesn't flow it's in danger of stagnating.

Its divinatory meanings are temperance, moderation, patience, accommodation, harmony, combining to make a perfect union, management, fusion, adjustment, consolidation, successful combination, beneficial influence, and accomplishment through self-control and frugality. It signifies a harmonious partnership, the healing effects of time, self-control, adaptability, and the assurance that peace will be restored after a troubled time. It teaches that we must first test the waters and never dive into a situation without thinking, to be patient and take things slowly, and to go carefully "where angels fear to tread."

Magically, Temperance symbolises that wishes will be fulfilled if the power of the imagination is expressed with balance and in harmony with our inner selves.

Sagittarians are recommended to carry one of these cards with them to illumine their paths, and to magnetise that for which they are asking. Go forth and claim the magic which is yours by using the symbolism of Temperance as your guide!

★ WHEEL OF FORTUNE ★
Ruled by Jupiter

Keywords ★ Change, Acceptance, Fate

★ KEY THEMES ★
A Miracle ★ Adjustment in Circumstances ★ A New Chapter ★ Changes in Fortune ★ Unexpected Turn of Events ★ Fate and Free Will ★ A Twist of Fate ★ Continual Movement ★ Responsibility for One's Own Destiny ★ Good luck ★ A Happy Accident ★ Balanced Karma ★ Destiny ★ Acceptance ★ Progress ★ Possibility to Intervene or Act ★

Fortuna, the Goddess of good luck's energy is inherent in the Wheel of Fortune card, and when this card appears in a reading, it means that:

"Fortune is indeed smiling on you and you may as well surrender to the flow, because something remarkable - a big event - is taking place. ... Although fate does not in any sense control our lives, when something has been wished for and worked

towards, it is the Goddess Fortuna who decides on the timing of the event. The Wheel of Fortune signifies a high point, a wish coming true, the manifestation of something anticipated."
***Mother peace: A Way to the Goddess Through Myth, Art and Tarot,* Vicky Noble, 1983**

Meditation ★ "I must take responsibility for my life to move forward in a positive direction"

Number ★ 10

Astrological Signs ★ Pisces, Sagittarius, & the Fixed Signs: Aquarius, Taurus, Leo and Scorpio

THE STORY ★ Tarot historians believe the word Tarot itself derives from the Latin word *rota*, as in 'rotation', and reflects the ancient sense of life as a moving wheel. The 'wheels within wheels' that make up the Wheel of Fortune, rotate and turn like the ever spinning rhythms and cycles of life. A spin of the wheel may bring unexpected luck, opportunity and good fortune, or it may cause the reverse, and present obstacles to our desires. A confrontation with some 'demon' from the past may occur with a turn of the wheel. These could be fate, part of a Divine plan, or karma, but what seem to be beginnings and endings are in fact just part of the never-ending circle of life. rising up from the horizon are two puffs of smoke that symbolise the form of spirit. In spite of all the changes, nothing remains but the elusive essence. Animals of varying characters and powers are depicted around the circle, and ultimately atop the wheel reigns a Sphinx, with flowing eyes that see all the cycles, evolutions, revolutions and recurring patterns. The Sphinx, in her quiet wisdom, knows that no one stays on top forever.

THE AWAKENING ★ It is not the Wheel of Fate but the Wheel of Fortune; this nuance is important. Indeed, the very fact that the wheel is activated by a handle, suggests the notion of free will at play. In other words, you have the choice to act or not to act, to use or not to use the handle in order to activate the wheel of your destiny. In any case, this card must prompt you to become aware of your share of active, conscious or unconscious responsibilities in the situations, circumstances or events we have to confront. Sometimes it indicates that we have to remain committed in order to progress; other times it means that for the moment, we can do nothing else but allow events to take their natural course. The turning of the Wheel of Fortune carries the message that what goes around, comes around, or what goes up, must come down. You will reap what you have sown, therefore you must think ahead and consider your actions today, wherever you find yourself on the wheel. To avoid being ruled by fate, take responsibility for your life and what happens in it. Be open to new and unexpected opportunities, allow for receiving, and above all, take risks. It is vitally important to always expect the unexpected. You must not worry about or fear the unexpected because it opens new perspectives for you.

THE LESSON ★ Ask your own spiritual guides or gods or goddesses to deliver to you your desires and just fortunes. Meditate on the Wheel of Fortune as you ask, and finally, take the chance and turn the wheel, for you never know where it may come to rest. The Wheel of Fortune represents the ability to understand and accept things, encouraging you to embrace changes in life wholeheartedly. There will always be highs and lows. Good or bad, trust that all is happening for your higher good. Accepting this brings a calmer, more holistic perspective.

SYMBOLISM *★ In Buddhist thought, the Wheel of Life is *Samsara*, the never-ending, going-nowhere spinning circle of illusion that represents the physical and emotional world of the senses. Buddhists believe the solution is to get off the Wheel by transcending these physical and emotional worlds. Some other religions and thoughts, suggest a coming to terms with the Wheel by understanding the laws of cause and effect, and by directing one's life accordingly.

The Wheel of Fortune symbolises the constant cycles that run through life. We may experience high and low points, yet the Wheel continues to turn. Therefore, the fundamental message of the Wheel is that you need to be attuned to the still centre within yourself, whatever the outer circumstances may be.

The Wheel of Fortune is turned by a blindfolded figure, looking in the opposite direction, symbolising that the ways of fate are a mystery and that you can only accept change, and work with it. The other figures, sitting on the Wheel and falling off as it turns, represent the varying experiences of life, and emphasise that resistance to change is completely futile.

Some Tarot decks depict the Wheel of Fortune as the Zodiac Wheel. This symbolism is quite apt, for just as we can do nothing about the turning of the stars in the sky, so we cannot avoid the turning of fate. This symbolism also suggests that we don't always have Earthly control over our fate and destiny. It further shows that there are higher laws set by a cosmic order.

Throughout history, the Wheel has been a potent image. In medieval times, when the Tarot first appeared, the Wheel represented not only the zodiac but also the cycle of birth and death, and the spinning wheel of the Fates. In this sense, the Wheel of Fortune denotes the uncertain nature of existence, as well as movement and change. Tarot historians believe the word Tarot itself derives from the Latin word *rota*, as in 'rotation', and reflects the ancient sense of life as a moving wheel.

This card signifies that a new chapter is beginning, a decision of importance is to be made, or that a new run of luck is commencing. The depiction of the turning Wheel of Fortune dates back to medieval times and, as a familiar Tarot image, it reveals four men who are attached to the wheel's rim. The goddess turning the wheel is blind, symbolising the element of chance that exists as fortunes of men rise and fall. The man at the top rules, the man descending has ruled, the man at the base of the wheel is without rule, while than man ascending will rule one day. Traditionally the card is said to be concerned with the beasts it portrays in some decks, and with the wheel itself; the Sphinx or Angel at the top says, "I rule," the serpent, "I have ruled," and the dog, "I will rule." (Other cards may have other animals aside from these, such as a monkey-like creature or jackal-headed man, and a hare. Some older decks still show two people celebrating together at the top of the wheel while a third man is hurled off the edge of a precipice. At the corners of some cards are figures: a bird, a lion, a bull and a human). These various depictions and meanings clearly reflect the ongoing peaks and troughs of life, and suggests that no one is exempt from a sudden change of fortune, be it for better or worse.

The Wheel of Fortune's association with the planet Jupiter links it with the transcendence of time, ruling the higher mind of Sagittarius and the devotion to intangibles of Pisces. Its divinatory meanings are destiny, fortune, fate, outcome, culmination, approaching the end of a problem, good or bad luck, depending on the influences of nearby cards, inevitability, a turn for the better, the end result of past actions and the workings of destiny, which no one can ever completely understand.

This card suggests the course of events from beginning to end, advancement for better or worse. It also signifies the end to current problems and some marked strokes of luck. But the Wheel of Fortune is a curious mix of fate and free will, as suggested by the wheel itself. The Wheel in some cards is kept in balance by a figure who sits at its top and aims to keep the equilibrium; she may or may not be successful. Two creatures are pictured trying to unbalance the wheel. They represent both positive progress and possible difficulties, denoting uncertainty - the Wheel could turn in either direction.

This card is the symbol of the paradox of stability and change. The true self of man, which is hidden from his conscious mind, very often remains at the still hub of the wheel, like the blindfolded goddess pictured in the centre of the wheel. The hub remains stable and represents the true self, although the external or conscious situations around it change, as reflected by the moving outer rim. Fate is the circumference of the wheel, and this true self is at the centre. The hub enables the rim to turn and therefore controls all that comes its way. It indicates that each man turns his own wheel to whichever point his true self dictates.

Overall, this card alludes to the mystic idea of karma, individual inner growth towards wholeness and harmony, symbolised by the circular mandala, and is a fortunate card, implying that your rightful destiny will unfold positively. Fortune is indeed smiling on you, and you may as well surrender to the flow, because something remarkable - a big event - is taking place. The Wheel of Fortune signifies a high point, a wish coming true, the manifestation of something anticipated. Ultimately, this card carries the message that the more aware you are of your own power over your destiny, the clearer things will appear - and that the wheel will turn in your favour eventually.

★ JUDGEMENT ★
Ruled by Pluto & the Element of Fire

Keywords ★ Evaluation, Opportunities, New Directions

★ KEY THEMES ★

★ Discernment ★ Karma ★ Reaping What Has Been Sown ★ Evaluation ★ Evolution ★ Review ★ Improvement ★ Revelation ★ Renewal ★ Favourable Assessment of the Facts ★ Objectivity ★ New Directions ★ Transformation ★ Legal Situations Resolved Favourably ★ Academic and Examination Success ★ Promotion ★ Bonus ★ A Career or Life Change ★ Moving in a Different Direction ★ Rehabilitation ★ Sound Decisions Based on Good Preparation and Evaluations ★ Recovery ★ Promotion ★ Admission of Guilt ★ Good News

Number ★ 20
Astrological Signs ★ Scorpio, Aries, Leo & Sagittarius

THE FOOL'S JOURNEY ★ Archetypically, Judgement means resurrection, the rebirth that comes with spiritual awareness and awakening. Arriving at this step on his journey, the Fool understands the possibilities of transformation that can come with change. The Fool reaches for enlightenment.

THE MESSAGE ★ Sometimes called the Angel, this card has a very simple but profound meaning - a second chance. Judgement portrays an end to suffering and the beginnings of a spiritual resurrection. Through Judgement, you are being offered a dissolution of negative past patterns and a resulting spiritual rebirth, the opportunity to review past events, and to offer forgiveness or make amends. Judgement symbolises a time of judgement, when souls rise from the dead to be judged. This card depicts an angel blowing a trumpet to awaken the dead from their graves, and announcing it is Judgement Day. Bodies emerge from their coffins with arms outstretched, often casting off funeral shrouds as they make ready to embrace the new life that is offered to them by the Angel of Judgement. There are usually three figures rising from the dead, to represent Mind, Body and Spirit, all of which must be brought forth to be judged. The dead are praying for mercy in the hope that the sins of their lifetimes will be forgiven. They now know that their misdemeanours are being exposed, and they are hoping to be allowed to move onto a higher plane of existence. On a spiritual wavelength, this card implies that one particular phase of your soul's journey is ending, and you will shortly assess what you learned and how you dealt with the passing situation, summing up your performance and its value to you. Judgment is telling you that at this point in your life it is time to assess and evaluate yourself, and perhaps address any underlying issues which up until now may have been ignored. To do this, you need simply to become more self-aware. Judgement emphasises that in undertaking this self-examination, you should be fair on yourself and focus on your positive character traits. It is telling you that once you have done this, like the symbolic people on the card, you will be ripe and ready to move in a new direction and onto a higher, more worthwhile plane of existence! You're either near the end of a project or at a crossroads, but either way, you are on the threshold of making an important change in your life.

THE STORY ★ The Judgement card is the respected mentor, who leads the way to a fresh perspective on life and leaves you feeling elated. Its main divinatory meanings are atonement, judgement, improvement, evaluation and finally, rebirth. In the symbolism of the Tarot, Judgement is not concerned with eternal damnation or heavenly bliss based upon this 'judgement' of your life experience so far, but instead with identifying ourselves the lessons we have learned not only from our archetypal Tarot journey so far, but through our whole life from birth onward. It is not a time for punishment and retribution, but a time of being called to account for past actions and experiences. After facing one's 'moment of truth', one can see oneself with more clarity and acceptance, and is then able to see others in the same way. This acceptance is an understanding of the human condition, human beauty, and embraces imperfections and Divine wisdom alongside each other. Our past, having been reflected upon, ensures that a positive resolution will be reinforced. With atonement and repentance, real advancement can occur. Therefore, Judgement is less about guilt and more about self-knowledge.

SYMBOLISM *★ Judgement brings you a new sense of Self. It renews and restores, and signifies that a rebirth process is taking place within the Self. A wider perspective has become available.

The angel in the card uses a trumpet, as if to call the figures from their sleepy sense of unawareness into full awakening. The cloud symbolises that this is spiritual in nature. The figures gradually rise - they are becoming released from the bonds of the past, and begin to look upwards towards an all-encompassing, broader and joyous perspective.

In some decks, the tombs are floating in a sea or river, which associates it with the notion that a river must be crossed before reaching the Promised Land. At the point of resurrection, evaluations must be made on each soul's life; therefore, this card portrays the need to reflect on life as it has been lived so far, to decide how one should proceed in the future.

This card's divinatory meanings are atonement, self-assessment, the need to repent or forgive, judgement, improvement, rebirth, rejuvenation, promotion, development, the desire for immortality, and the moment to account for the manner in which we have used our opportunities on our life's journey thus far. The Judgement card may also signify the final settlement of a matter, and a time to pay off old debts in preparation for a fresh beginning. It suggests that that which has been lying dormant will spring to life, as symbolised by the dead rising from their coffins. Judgement also indicates that the rewards for past efforts will soon finally be forthcoming.

The word 'judgement', derived from the Latin *judicem*, means 'to show or to speak what is right'. But in the context of this card, is has another meaning: discernment. As far as Judgement is concerned, discernment takes the form of distinction, recognition and separation, and all that can be accomplished. The people in the card standing beneath the figure, wearing only their nakedness, show themselves as they are, stripped of any artifice. The light within may therefore now shine forth and they no longer have any need to feel ashamed of their nudity, or to be themselves. They can discriminate between what is true or false, just or unjust. The information that has shaped their existence and made them live in hope or in fear no longer comes from external sources, but from an internal wellspring - from *themselves*. This is a revelation. For we are all assailed by outside forces which are often unconnected with our lives, that leave us feeling powerless and depressed. With such hubbub and chaos surrounding us, it is hard to hear our inner voice (depicted as the angel on this card) and see and feel the light of our own wisdom (represented by the rays of the Sun around the angel). If we cannot hear these things, how can we detect, dissect and discern? Indeed, Judgement foretells a revelation, a renewal, an inner vision that is more accurate, more profound, more objective and real. Its presence suggests that we can no longer lie to ourselves or hide the truth from others, bringing a relief, a cure, a reconciliation, a state of trust, a relaxing of tenseness, and total receptivity. It can also reveal a vocation, a promotion, a recognition or a reward that comes about as a result of our newfound inner consultations.

The Judgement card indicates that the time is ripe for a period of self-appraisal, which involves taking an honest look at yourself, your motivations and your actions. This means reviewing your accomplishments so far, neither under- or over-valuing them. It also advises that one should carefully consider how present actions affect others around them.

Ultimately, Judgement suggests that it is time to review, assess, evaluate and make some considered and thoughtful judgements regarding your life, and then make empowered decisions. To put it another way, in the words of Henry David Thoreau: "Go confidently in the direction of your dreams. Live the life you have imagined." It is time to practice discernment and then move in a new direction, from that newfound, redeemed, freed spirit.

* Please note that the images described are not found in all Tarot decks. The images in different decks can differ considerably.

THE TAROT'S SUIT OF WANDS ★ REPRESENTING THE FIRE ELEMENT

The Tarot Wands (known in some old decks as Rods, Staves or Batons) are connected with growth, creativity, enterprise, ambition, progress, initiative, work/labour, action, adventure, energy, vitality, willpower, reputation, fame, efficiency, achievement, challenge and all creative matters. The Wands represent the Fire element, and their Fire is mainly influenced by the planet Mars, which activates travel and work energy, and sexual force, but they also partake the energies of Jupiter - the Fire of benevolent warmth and expansion - and incorporate the Fire of the Sun, radiating confidence and wellbeing in all directions. Being of the Fire realm, the Wands are also associated with dynamic action, inspiration, passion and determination. Like fire itself, they signify the ignition and generation of warmth and energy, while also burning off the dross and impurities of life. Fire creates light and heat, but it can too readily burn and easily rage out of control, which can lead to destruction, ruin and havoc. However, the energy of Fire can also be transformative. It needs fuel in order to be effective, and if this vital fuel is sourced only from the feelings, flames can be swiftly burned out. Therefore, the ultimate source of fuel for this brand of Fire lies within the self's sense of connection with the spirit - as this is a deep well that never runs dry.

The narrative of the fiery Suit of Wands propels you forward and defines your actions and motivations in life. It tells of the need to create change and movement, always beginning with the initial spark that sets the flames of passion ablaze. If Wands predominate in a reading, there's a high chance you are actively engaged in accomplishing your goals. They deal with the physical and spiritual life force - positive conflict, struggle and passion all being part of its expression. They reveal how active, dynamic, enthusiastic and passionate we are, and how these are experienced and expressed by us. There are often elements of struggle with the Wands suit, because energy needs to move freely and spontaneously, and any blockages to this have to be shifted. Conflicts within the Wands cards are generally not considered serious, and lead to a deeper, more profound sense of Self once they are resolved. They also govern inspiration and the spark that can appear out of the blue to light the way forward. In a deck of playing cards, the Wands correspond to the suit of Clubs.

THE LUCKY 13 ★ SAGITTARIAN TIPS FOR INCREASED MAGIC, LUCK & MAGNETISM

1 ★ Incorporate Sagittarian symbols into your daily life to remind yourself of your soul's mission.

2 ★ Use the crystal Topaz in any form in your daily life - wear it, meditate with it, hold it and carry it with you everywhere! Topaz it is an excellent stone to use for attraction and manifestation purposes, attracting people to you on friendship, love and business levels, and manifesting your desires as long as they are for the greater good. Topaz has the power to magnetise prosperity, honour, glory and recognition of your worth, and is an empathetic stone that directs energy to where it is needed most. It soothes, heals, recharges, stimulates, re-motivates, and aligns the meridians of the body, enhancing emotions and states of being that can assist in attracting wonderful things to you.

3 ★ Wear or surround yourself with the colours purple, royal blue, azure and indigo.

4 ★ Learn the way of the Twins. Gemini has much to teach the Sagittarian soul. Stop trying to break free from the reins and enjoy the moment … Learn simpler applications … Roam the lower planes … Gather facts and trivia for the mere enjoyment of it … Think purity and perfection … Get back in touch with your inner child … Stop trying to save the world and save yourself instead ... Celebrate and appreciate the little details of life ... Enjoy a fearless love affair for the fun of it ... Learn some silly pieces of pointless information to share with others ... Go to a party and make small talk; not everything has to be discussed in depth - the weather is a great place to start ... Throw a fancy dress party and make it a children's theme ... it's *all* within you!

5 ★ Use your lucky numbers 3 and 9 whenever you are needing an extra stroke of luck.

6 ★ Magnify and celebrate your independence, freedom of spirit, powerful intellect, philosophical views and idealism. You can use them to great benefit as you quest towards the ever-present but never-quite-reachable horizon!

7 ★ Remind yourself of your mission constantly, that is by speaking, breathing and *truly living* your dreams and insights - give them form beyond simply idealising or philosophising about them!

8 ★ Focus your energies on exploring your higher mind, spiritual evolution and beliefs, and transforming yourself through your intellectual faculties - which are strongly accessible to the acutely seeking, receptive, expansive and ever-evolving Sagittarian mind. Connect with your deep wisdom and inborn creative spark through any means possible.

9 ★ Use your innate powers of global awareness, pure faith and belief in the unseen, and metaphysical attunement to visualise and draw that which you desire towards you. If you can develop simple faith in the positive outcome of events, you can easily use your keen intuition to great creative effect.

10 ★ Tap into and utilise your ability to guide, teach, share, exchange, give to and transform others through sharing your emotions, spirit and soul. But to do that, you'll need to ease yourself off your cloud and back onto planet Earth where the rest of us reside! We need you here at least some of the time!

11 ★ View your idealistic nature as a strength and call forth the powers of your generous, insightful gifted, unique self. Be who you *really* are, without reservation or apology, and the rest will fall into place.

12 ★ Become the 'Philosophical Enlightener' of others - and yourself - that you were born to be!

13 ★ Once you have mastered purer focus for your ideals, greater direction, and a supreme aim with your arrow, learn to share the resulting abundance, insights and knowledge with others so they too can walk the Higher Path!

HAVE YOU PACKED YOUR MAGICAL BAG FOR THE JOURNEY?

If you wish to increase and draw more luck, love and abundance into your life, a power pack is essential. For Sagittarians, I would recommend carrying or wearing the following items on you on your travels. Then just sit back and watch as magic pours into your experiences and realities, both inner and outer!

★ One of each of the following gemstones: Topaz, Turquoise, Zircon, Yellow Sapphire, Amethyst
★ Tarot cards Temperance and Wheel of Fortune (and the Judgement card too, if you wish)
★ An elk in any form (use your imagination!)
★ Something made of tin
★ An arrowhead symbol in any form
★ A postcard or image from a hot, dry place (representing your Choleric disposition). Bon Voyage!
★ A postcard from the future to yourself, proclaiming, 'Wish You Were Here!'

A FINAL WORD ★ TAPPING INTO THE MAGIC OF SAGITTARIUS

There is something inherently magical about Sagittarius, the enchanting Archer. Blessed with an unrivalled faith in the spiritual forces, a brilliant mind and a dazzling philosophical outlook, they truly are the Magical Adventurers of the zodiac, affecting everyone around them with their free-spirited charm and easy going wit. Never malicious but ever tactless and direct, the Sagittarius seeks to broaden the mind through travel in all its forms: mind, body, soul and spirit. To really tap into your true magic, this connection with your higher purpose is imperative to your life's spring of wellbeing. You also need to honour your personal freedom and never allow yourself to be stifled or held back from your dreams. You are the sign of the idealist. Connect! Exchange! Expand! Embrace! Philosophise! Be free! Teach! Preach! Shine!

Nothing is subtle or pessimistic about you. The cosmos has endowed you with the precious and important gifts of generosity, optimism, curiosity, wanderlust, vision, far-sightedness, enthusiasm, benevolence, and a wholehearted sense of wonder and hope. Whether you are fully cognisant of it or not, a magical reservoir of energy is available to you to tap into whenever it is needed.

Finally, to attune yourself to luck, harmony and success, Sagittarians should wear, eat, inhale, meditate upon, create, design, and dance with any or all of the suggested luck-enhancers for your Sun sign to receive the most beneficial astral vibrations these 'boosters' can offer you. Wearing, decorating and working with the amazing powers of all your lucky guides, animals, crystals, colours, woods, cards, herbs, foods, places, talismans, planetary influences, charms, numbers, and other magical tips contained within the words of this very book, will bring you greater abundance, love, magic, energy, happiness and personal power, and attract all manner of things to you like bees to sweet flowers. This, my Sagittarian friends, I promise you - and Aquarians *never* lie.

Good luck on the rest of your amazing life journey, and may the LUCK be with you!

Lani is also available for personal Astrology, Numerology, Aura * & Tarot reading consultations, via post, email, Skype and in-person. Please email lalana76@bigpond.com for more information.

In-person only

Facebook Page ★ Astrology Magic

Other Books in the **Lucky Astrology** Series

Lucky Astrology ★ Aries
Lucky Astrology ★ Taurus
Lucky Astrology ★ Gemini
Lucky Astrology ★ Cancer
Lucky Astrology ★ Leo
Lucky Astrology★ Virgo
Lucky Astrology ★ Libra
Lucky Astrology ★ Scorpio
Lucky Astrology ★ Capricorn
Lucky Astrology ★ Aquarius
Lucky Astrology ★ Pisces

Order your copies now, from White Light Publishing House, at www.whitelightpublishingau.com

www.ingramcontent.com/pod-product-compliance
Lightning Source LLC
Chambersburg PA
CBHW071155300426
44113CB00009B/1215